The Third Year of
THE
Nixon Watch

The Third Year of
THE
Nixon Watch

BY

JOHN OSBORNE

Illustrated by PAT OLIPHANT

LIVERIGHT

NEW YORK

E
855
.0814

LIVERIGHT

1.987654321

This book consists of articles that appeared in *The New Republic* between January 1971 and January 1972. The title is derived from "The Nixon Watch," the standing head under which John Osborne reports the Presidency for that magazine. Apart from some changes of tense for present clarity, the correction of typographical and similar errors, and the addition of updating addenda at the ends of a few chapters, the originals have not been altered for this publication. All articles are reprinted by permission of the publisher.

International Standard Book Number: 0–87140–551–2
Library of Congress Catalog Card Number: 73–184101
Printed in the United States of America

CONTENTS

The Third Year of
THE
Nixon Watch

I

Notes from a Nightmare

Here are some thoughts and points about Mr. Nixon and his Presidency, mostly derived from his televised conversation with four network luminaries on January 4 and from interviews at the White House during the preceding fortnight.

At a Cabinet meeting on the morning after the TV session, the President said he was disappointed that several questions that he had been prepared to answer had not been asked. He was disappointed with the conversation before it occurred. The assistants who arranged it for him had indicated that he hoped for reflective questions that would invite reflective answers about himself, the Presidency and its problems, the processes by which he arrived at his decisions. The reaction of the regular White House press corps to these intimations doomed his hopes. A suspicion arose that the affair was framed, that the chosen conversationalists would be debarred from putting hard questions that went to the gut of the news and would be expected to serve up what reporters call "soft-balls." The four questioners demanded and got assurances from Press Secretary Ronald Ziegler and Communications Director Herbert Klein that no restrictions were intended or implied. In the event, they demonstrated their journalistic virility with hard queries that elicited less interesting information than the few reflective questions did.

It's not often that a President, called upon to say how and whether two years in office have changed him, admits that he knew less about the office than he needed to know when he assumed it and that now "I know more. I'm better. I'm more experienced. I hope to do better." Reminded of his promise in early 1968 to give the country "the lift of a driving dream," and agreeing that he had failed to fulfill it, the President recalled "the nightmares" of assassination, domestic violence and a hated war that haunted his first two years and said, "You can't be having a driving dream when you are in the midst of a nightmare." There was a touch here of synthetic apology, as there was in his remark that his questioners wouldn't want to be caught "being soft on Nixon" (this with the famous cringing smile), and in his attempt to equate the student killings at Kent State University and Jackson State College with the student bombing at the University of Wisconsin. Generally, however, he was at his effective best when he was allowed to turn from the news to the problems behind the news—including the problem that is Richard Nixon himself.

His senior assistants would do well to ponder one such reply. Nothing antagonizes them toward reporters more than any suggestion that Mr. Nixon is in less firm command of himself on some occasions than he is on others. Howard Smith of ABC observed that the President had said in his book, *Six Crises,* that in periods following tension and crisis he had to guard against faulty reactions and judgments. Smith asked whether "you think you have mastered that aftermath period now." Mr. Nixon replied that a man who has been through what he has been through gets to a point where he "paces himself properly" and knows of himself that "in a moment of let-down he might make a mistake." The President then said: "I don't mean that I've mastered it completely, because I would be the first to admit that I'm just as human as anybody else."

In discussing himself and his hopes and plans for the second two years of his present term, the President said much that various members of his staff had said lately about him and his attitudes.

The thrust of their accounts had been that he genuinely did expect the coming biennium to be "a great two years" and that he was enjoying the difficult choices that had to be made before he came up with his 1971 State of the Union, Budget and legislative messages and proposals. If so, the pleasure was of fairly recent origin. His televised acknowledgment that progress toward his goals in the first two years had been less than he hoped for, and his indications that in the coming two years he would deal differently with Congress, with his Cabinet, and with his national constituency coincided indirectly but in an interesting way with the analysis offered by one of his more objective assistants.

After the 1970 campaign and elections, with a net outcome clearly short of the enormous success that the President had declared it to be, it seemed to this assistant that Mr. Nixon went through a time of rather puzzled frustration, of wondering how and why it was that so much of the electorate had failed to respond as he expected to his initiatives and programs and to his campaign pleas for support. At first, the post-election word to everybody on the White House staff had been to follow the Presidential line of a great success; and then, very suddenly and very firmly, to shut up and say nothing more to outsiders about the election results. Whether this meant that Mr. Nixon himself had reconsidered, the assistant didn't know and didn't know of anybody else at the White House who knew. But he sensed that the President, behind his show of enhanced toleration for Democratic critics and dissident Republicans, was at least for the time being more impatient with and less tolerant of such characters than he had previously been. If this analysis was correct, and I suspect that it was, we saw in the January 4 conversation and on other recent occasions a President in the act of putting on a masterly act, all the more impressive because it concealed some of his true feelings.

Mr. Nixon in late 1970 asked the principal members of his staff for memoranda setting forth their ideas of how he should conduct himself in 1971. A common and not particularly insightful view, reflected by the President on television, was that he should appear to regard 1971 as "a nonpolitical year" and defer outward political activities and concerns until 1972. Mr. Nixon understood that he was being urged to engage in a charade and thought it was rather funny ("Why," he said in a mocking tone to one of his congressional leaders, "you don't think I'd be thinking *politically,* do you?"). But he bought it, and one of the results was that his friend and associate from his early California days, Murray Chotiner, was told to look around for a job well away from the White House staff. There were thoughts of placing him at the Republican National Committee, provided that its new chairman, unlike outgoing Chairman Rogers Morton, is willing to put up with so close and trusted a Nixon surrogate at his elbow. Chotiner's departure, when announced, was intended to be one of several signals that in 1971 the President was forgoing the delights of what one assistant called "frontal politics." The same assistant said that Harry Dent, Chotiner's fellow-specialist in hard-line politics and the President's personal emissary to Southern Republicans, was to be kept on at the White House, head well down but quietly at work as usual on the finer nuances of the Southern Strategy.

Unbeknownst to some of the closest associates of the President and of the assistant in question, Mr. Nixon was assured only at the turn of the year that Henry A. Kissinger would be staying with him for a while. Amid the recent flurry of Staff and Cabinet changes, the general assumption has been that the President's assistant for national security affairs was too enamored of the power and prominence associated with his job to leave it for a return to Harvard, whence he came, or perhaps for some other university faculty. The assumption was wrong until very recently, and in the first week of January it still was not completely sound. Mr. Nixon told Kissinger last September or thereabouts that he, the President, wanted him to remain through the second half of the term and Kissinger said that he would think about it. He thought about it well into December, in the meantime acquiring private assurances at Harvard that he would find an acceptable spot waiting for him if he decided to stay with Mr. Nixon beyond the expiration of his two-year leave in January and chose to return to the university later in 1971. His understanding with the President in early January was that he would indeed remain, but not necessarily for the whole of the next two years. From now on, he is at the White House on an until-further-notice basis and that apparently is all right with the President. I am told and believe that there is no question of disagreement on any ground between

Kissinger and the President; it's merely, I gather, that Henry Kissinger's well known and well developed vanity has been widely misinterpreted. The prevalent notion that it binds him to the White House and to the eminence that goes with his job there offends him. He prefers to have it understood that he is quite capable of surrendering his share of Presidential power and going back to the academy.

January 16, 1971

———

Murray Chotiner, who was among those who recommended that the President appear to regard 1971 as a "non-political year," joined a Washington law firm. For the resolution of Henry Kissinger's doubts about staying on, see Chapter X.

Secretary Richardson

One of Elliot Richardson's assistants, watching him on a TV panel show, turned to another assistant and groaned, "Oh God, there's our man again, coming over like a codfish on ice." This was said in mingled pain, bafflement, and affection. The Secretary of Health, Education, and Welfare comes over to his admirers at the department and to White House officials who work with him as a warm and witty fellow and, what is more, as a genius at public administration who could be President if presidents were elected on the basis of sheer ability and intellect. Richardson gives many other people, this reporter among them, an impression of great competence and of a desire to use that competence for the public good. But those who esteem him, whether they be advocates in his service or friendly journalists, have two difficulties. One of the difficulties is with his record, which seems to be rather bare of concrete and citable accomplishments. The other difficulty is with Richardson himself. He simply does not convey to the public, and he is not very good at conveying to individuals whom he doesn't know well, the qualities of warmth and humor that are said to leaven and contradict the codfish image.

President Nixon arrived the hard way at his present liking for Richardson. Although they knew each other in 1956–58, when Richardson was an Assistant Secretary of HEW, Nixon was not prepared for one of Richardson's quirks when he first became Under Secretary of State in 1969 and attended occasional meetings at the White House. Richardson is a doodler. In his own office, at Cabinet meetings and even (to the horror of his staff) in the President's office, he holds a large notepad in front of himself, just below face level, and doodles away, glancing up from his swirls and squares and circles within squares only when a remark catches his interest or he is impelled to say something. When he isn't doodling, he is making notes on another sheet of paper. The habit intimidates and annoys people who aren't accustomed to it. A story heard at the White House early in the Administration had it that Nixon was so annoyed that he told Secretary of State William P. Rogers to keep that man away from him. Rogers was said to have explained that it was Richardson's way of concentrating on the business in hand, not of ignoring it, and that no rudeness was meant. Nixon soon welcomed Richardson back to Presidential councils and came to share the opinion that he did a standout job of administering the State Department and of bringing its policy processes into harmony with the White House processes established by Henry Kissinger.

When the President replaced Robert Finch with Richardson at HEW and brought Finch to the White House staff last June, he said he did it partly because that huge and historically unmanageable department needed a strong administrator. The aftermath illustrates the difficulty of determining what Richardson has actually *done* to justify his impressive reputation. A natural question was what difference his departure from State made in its operations and in its working relationships with the White House, in both of which Richardson was supposed to have been a key figure. The answer given at State and at the White House was that Richardson's departure has made no discernible difference; that things went along under his successor at State, a New York lawyer named John N. Irwin II who qualifies as the Administration's invisible man, just about as they had under Richardson. A similar difficulty is encountered at HEW. After six months of the Richard-

son regime, the talk heard in his behalf there is mostly of what
he intends to do and is trying to do to bring his department, which
he rightly calls "a great coalition," into some sort of cohesive
institutional order, with a sense of institutional entity that it has
lacked ever since it was thrown together in 1954.

That alone is a major undertaking and the larger purpose that
Richardson has in mind is even more formidable. The larger purpose, which Richardson has yet to find a way to articulate with
total coherence, is to persuade HEW's 100,000-plus employes and
the heads and chief operatives in its 57 divisions, agencies, bureaus
and offices that they are hired and exist to serve *people,* rather
than simply to devise and implement programs in welfare, health,
education that may or may not really serve the people they are
intended to serve. It is even more complicated than the foregoing
paraphrase of Richardson's many attempts to state his purposes
may indicate. HEW's function consists largely of doling out money,
in forms ranging from Social Security payments to hundreds of
various kinds of grants to states, localities and private agencies
which actually serve or fail to serve the poor, the sick, the students
at the end of the long federal line. One of Richardson's endeavors
is to distinguish those functions which are or could be solely and
simply "resource transfer" activities from those that require federal
control or guidance of the uses to which the money is put and to
concentrate the department's energies and powers upon the latter.
He speaks with scorn of what he calls the "Don't just stand there,
do something syndrome," holding that it has led his department
to waste much of its talents and time upon niggling and unnecessary controls that should be left to the subsidized state, local
or private agencies that deliver the actual services.

Here, however, he runs into more difficulty. He prefers a minimum of federal supervision of the delivered services, and he is
profoundly distrustful of the notion that the setting of federal
standards and the direct enforcement of them can or ever will
resolve the many deficiencies and variations in the services delivered by subsidized agencies. He speaks of "goals" rather than
"standards," of "incentives" rather than direct federal compulsion.
He argues in essence that the basic and feasible federal task is
somehow to "communicate" to the non-federal components of the
vast social-service complex a desire to reach high and agreed

"goals" and to provide them with the federal funds, knowledge and expertise that they may need to attain effective levels of delivery and performance. Any suggestion that this philosophy calls for a degree of confidence in the good faith and inherent competence of state and local governments that the record hardly justifies causes Richardson obvious pain. "I guess I will have to start over," he says, and does, leaving one with the impression that he is willing to use federal power in a positive way to accomplish federal purposes when it is proven to be absolutely necessary.

One place where the Richardson approach is perfectly understood and appreciated is the White House. Nobody there is willing to draw comparisons between one Cabinet Secretary and another, but the inquirer gets the impression that Elliot Richardson qualifies as Mr. Nixon's ideal department head. He has adjusted with complete grace and composure to changes in the traditional relationship between Presidents and Cabinet members that in times past and in a less disciplined Administration would have brought about open revolt. One of the changes, imposed by the President last summer, deprived department heads of their right of personal appeal to him on disputed budget issues. Apart from rare group meetings with the President, they were required in preparing the upcoming fiscal 1972 budget to deal entirely with John D. Ehrlichman, the assistant for domestic affairs and director of the Domestic Council, and with George P. Shultz, director of the Office of Management and Budget. There came a time, very late in the budget process, when Richardson reduced his department's alternative allocations to 10 points that, as recently as 1969, the Secretary concerned would have expected as a matter of right to take up with the President. Richardson took them up with Shultz, worked them out to the satisfaction of both men, and never went near the President.

Richardson concluded in late December of 1970 that only the President could decide between some of the competing options, worked out principally at HEW, for the new national health insurance system that Mr. Nixon has billed as one of his top domestic proposals for 1971. If the President made the choices, he did it through Ehrlichman, who had Richardson reduce the alternatives to a brief memo and handled all of the personal discussion with the Secretary. Richardson says that these experiences and others like them gave him no sense that he is excluded from the President. If that's the way Mr. Nixon wants it, that's the way Richardson wants it. It's the way to thrive in this Administration.

January 23, 1971

III

Call It Desegregation

At the White House, where modest and often dubious claims of Administration achievement are regularly trumpeted, the President and his spokesmen didn't say a word on January 14 and in the week thereafter about figures documenting one of Mr. Nixon's real successes. The ignored subject was the progress achieved in the fall of 1970 in the desegregation of Southern public schools. Figures announced on the 14th by HEW Secretary Elliot Richardson showed that some 80 percent of school-age black children in 11 Southern states were in public schools that white children also attended. The proportion (38.2 percent) of black children in public schools where most of the pupils were white was higher in the South than it was anywhere else in the country. Overall, there was less segregated public schooling in the South than in the North and West. In short, the figures appeared to document the Administration's claim that the South's traditional system of dual and officially segregated public schools had been to all effects dismantled. On their face, with every discount for the reality behind the statistics, they demonstrated that the issues and the problems involved in school desegregation had changed fundamentally and for the better, and that the change had come to a climax in the first two years of Mr. Nixon's Administration.

Secretary Richardson spoke with reason of the "dramatic and unprecedented progress" indicated by his statistics. But his was the sole note of official jubilation, and his total treatment of the facts at a press conference was restrained. Attorney General John N. Mitchell, a principal architect of the Administration's de-segregation policy and tactics, barely mentioned the matter in a biennial review of his department's record. It was as if the Admin-istration would rather have skipped the whole thing, and there should have been no wonder if it had. The Nixon success was not the degree of formal desegregation that had been accomplished in the South, a process that the President had taken great pains to credit more to the courts than to his own policy and actions. His success was in cozening the white South, in his 1968 campaign for the Presidency and again in the midterm 1970 campaign, into believing that he as President would do what he could to slow if not prevent the completion of the very process that was now, on the face of his Administration's figures, much nearer completion than critics of his social policies had thought likely or possible. Viewed politically, and that was the way Mr. Nixon naturally viewed it, the resultant situation was downright funny. His own exercise in constructive deception debarred him from claiming any-thing near full and personal credit for its success, for to do so would have been to confess the deception and thereby to alienate white Southern votes that he and the Republican Party will need to win in 1972. He may be expected now and in the future, as he has done since 1968, to say that his Administration in this matter does only what Congress and the courts require it to do, and to allot the remainder of the credit, as Secretary Richardson did on the 14th, to "the way in which people in the South—black and white alike—have carried out the requirements of the law."

The Administration's current prayer to Congress and to the Supreme Court, expressed in veiled but unmistakable terms, is that "the requirements of the law" not be broadened so as to prohibit segregated schooling that results from residential and other cir-cumstances, rather than from deliberate official action. It is upon the hope that enforceable law and court rulings will continue to be limited to deliberate (*de jure*) rather than to circumstantial (*de facto*) segregation and related racial discrimination that HEW and the Department of Justice base their present posture and their plans to apply the law as it stands in the South and elsewhere. The South still has its own special and aggravated racial problems in its public schools. But the essence of the change signalled by the 1970 figures is that the enforcement problem there is coming to be identical with the problem in the rest of the nation, and that, in a real sense, the problem is even harder to solve than it had been in the 16 years since the Supreme Court ruled that deliberate segregation of public schools by race violates the Constitution.

Secretary Richardson acknowledged that segregated schools, segregated classrooms, and the most outrageous racial discrimination can and do exist within formally desegregated school systems and that, where they are proven to result from deliberate official action, the federal government is obligated to put an end to them. He cited the firing and demotion of black teachers in desegregating Southern systems and schools as one of the obvious and widespread abuses subject to federal penalty; he has had his department's enforcement agency, the Office for Civil Rights, notify school authorities they must treat black and white teachers alike if they are "to remain eligible for federal funds." He has instructed OCR to go into the field and "make a case" wherever complaints or known circumstances suggest that there is a case to be made. The Secretary means it; he is acting in good faith. Yet, given literally hundreds of complaints and other causes for remedial action, his department has moved in only three cases since he took charge of it last summer to terminate the payment of federal funds to offending school districts. One of the reasons is that the Administration, following a policy designed by Attorney General Mitchell, prefers to sue recalcitrant school districts instead of cutting off their federal money by administrative action. The effect and the purpose are to turn public ire from the Administration to the courts and so to minimize the political costs of desegregation. But a corollary fact, as Administration apologists will be arguing from now on, is that "making the case" really does become more and more difficult as formal and declared segregation recedes. The motives behind such practices as the dismissal and demotion of black teachers in the course of reducing desegregated teaching staffs and the in-school grouping of black and white students on the basis

of standard scholastic tests have to be proven to the satisfaction of
judges and administrators alike, and adequate proof of that kind
can be extremely hard to come by.

Stating the difficulties that arise from the changing patterns of
segregation and discrimination does not, of course, establish an
excuse for delay and passivity in the enforcement of statutory and
judicial law. The case against the attitudes and behavior that survive in much of the South, and against the Administration's recent
and actual approach to them, is devastating in both detail and
effect. Two studies of Southern school discrimination and federal
action to deal with it were conducted last fall by the Washington
Research Project and five national organizations concerned with
civil rights. The studies proved beyond question what journalists
and others familiar with the subject already knew: that the $75
million in emergency school funds appropriated by Congress last
fall, ostensibly to further Southern desegregation in the 1970–71
school year, was intended to be used and was used primarily as
a straight payoff for minimal compliance with the law. President Nixon's personal order was to "get that money out there"
and it was gotten "out there," as often as not in flagrant disregard
of the nominal requirement that school districts receiving it abandon or correct any and all forms of racial discrimination in their
schools. Forty of 109 complaints that were checked by the Office
for Civil Rights were found to be justified, and the offending districts were asked to correct the violations without forcing HEW
or Justice to take formal action. The plea heard in private from
federal administrators is that the combination of deception, per-
suasion and positive enforcement in cases of last resort has worked
and is still working, to the extent demonstrated by the federal
statistics. So it has and is, with the odd result that Mr. Nixon and
his Administration neither care nor dare to claim the credit that
in another atmosphere and in other circumstances would be their
due.

January 30, 1971

IV

Revolution or Reversal?

Eight of Mr. Nixon's assistants spent January 22 telling scores of journalists why they should pay respectful heed to the President's call for a "new American revolution." At group and individual briefings, in the most extensive and intensive effort of the kind that has occurred at the Nixon White House, the chief reason advanced by the President's men for taking the State of the Union message with the utmost seriousness was neither the grandeur of his "six great goals" nor his proposals for massive reorganization of the federal government and for expanded sharing of federal revenues with state and local governments. The chief reason offered was that the message and the legislative programs promised in it expressed a definite philosophy of government, a philosophy to which Mr. Nixon was deeply committed and which he was determined to make the nation's philosophy. Don't get lost in details that you can't have for a while anyway, the Nixon briefers kept telling reporters and commentators. Don't fog the issue with questions that can't be answered right now. Just stick to the main point, which is the philosophy, and try to grasp it and convey it to readers and listeners.

That injunction came over loud and clear. What didn't come over so well was the philosophy. The briefers and Mr. Nixon when he delivered his message had the trouble that all New Federalists have when they try to present and justify their doctrine as an actionable philosophy of government. During and before the 1968 campaign, Mr. Nixon had no trouble with such statements as, "The time has come to reverse the flow of power from the states and communities to Washington," and "What we need now is a dispersal of power—so there is not one center of power, but many centers." Assertions of this sort and the accompanying qualifications—"I am not saying the federal government should back off from its responsibilities"—then had the honest and hollow ring of campaign simplicities. The trouble comes, as it came to Mr. Nixon in his State of the Union speech, when the contradiction has to be reconciled. Two of his White House writers, William Safire and Tom Huston, demonstrated this when they, with the President's assent, wrote and privately circulated two papers last year, respectively setting forth and criticizing the contradictory principles of the New or Nixon Federalism. Safire's advocacy of what he called "national localism" and Huston's critique of it seemed to me to be equally opaque, but Mr. Nixon was said to admire both documents as useful expositions and examinations of his philosophy. The exchange between "Publius" (Safire) and "Cato" (Huston), under pseudonyms borrowed from the original Federalist Papers, is cited at the White House now as evidence that the philosophy expounded by the President in his message was not something cooked up for the occasion or for some such invidious purpose as putting the Democratic Congress on the spot in 1972 if it failed to enact Mr. Nixon's proposals.

The proposals, his "six great goals," included the welfare reform that died in the last Congress; a modest national health program that will require more federal effort than federal money; environmental protections that also call for a minimum of federal expenditure; and adherence by Congress to the limits set by the President on his "expansionary" budget (with an estimated deficit of $18.5 billion this fiscal year, $11.6 billion in fiscal 1972). His and his preparatory briefers' big pitch, however, was for federal reorganization and for a very substantial enlargement of his previous un-

THE PROOF OF THE PUDDING . . . .

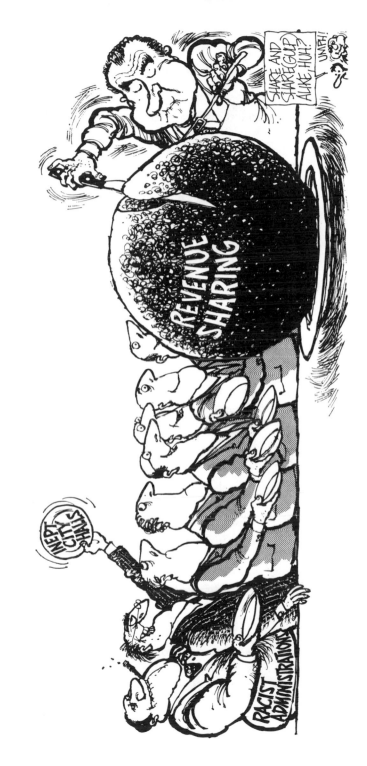

dertaking to share federal revenues with states and localities. The press was told again and again, and Mr. Nixon told the senators and representatives who streamed to the White House during the week following the message, that these proposals were the absolute essentials of his 1971 program. These, it was said, were the measures needed above all others to make a reality of the President's admonition to "put the money where the needs are" and "put the power to spend it where the people are."

His proposal to abolish seven federal departments (Health, Education, and Welfare; Housing and Urban Development; Interior, Agriculture, Commerce, Labor, and Transportation) and to regroup their functions, along with some independent agency functions, into four huge departments named for and "organized around" four "great purposes of government" (Human Resources, Natural Resources, Community Development and Economic Development) called on its face for enormous concentrations of federal power. Mr. Nixon acknowledged no contradiction between this prospect and his call for a dispersal of federal power. On the contrary, he argued that it would "focus and concentrate the responsibility for getting problems solved" in collaboration with refreshed and invigorated state and local governments.

The refreshment and invigoration would come from the shared federal money and the freedom in its use that would go with it to state and local governments. The sharing would take two forms, one a genuine innovation and the other not so genuine. Federal revenue amounting to a fixed proportion (1.3 percent) of the nation's total taxable personal income would be returned each year to states and localities. The only conditions limiting its use would be that states and localities share it according to a federally set formula (on average, 52 percent to the states and 48 percent to localities) and that federal laws and regulations prohibiting racial and other discrimination be observed. The base percentage would produce $5 billion for "general sharing" in the first full year of operation, more in years when total personal income increases.

The companion "special revenue sharing" would in fact be a sharing of funds that states and localities already get in the form of federal grants made according to predetermined federal criteria and expended under varying degrees of federal control. The aided governments would no longer have to match the federal money with their own (usually 10 to 30 percent of the total). With some extra money ($1 billion, the briefers said; $700 million, the 1972 budget message said), the conversion of these "categorical grants" to the more-or-less free grants proposed by the President would come to $11 billion for states and localities in the first complete fiscal year.

The fiscal 1972 budget message, published a week after Nixon spoke, disclosed some interesting details about this part of revenue sharing. Most of the converted grant programs would be in the social areas (education, urban renewal, model cities, community action) that now give the federal government the most trouble and entail the most stringent restrictions upon the use of the granted money for intended purposes in nondiscriminatory ways.

Contradictions even sharper than the overall contradiction between federal responsibility and state-local initiative studded the initial explanations and claims. The point emphasized by the President and his spokesmen was that benefited states and localities would have much more responsibility than they are permitted today for deciding both what to do with the grant money and how to use it. In the same breath, the Administration promised to forbid its use except for the general purposes stipulated in the grants and in violation of any and all federal prohibitions against the discriminatory use of it. Scandalous misuse of granted funds, for example of the large sums intended only to improve the schooling of poor and disadvantaged children, has been exposed and proven many times. Mr. Nixon will find, as one may suspect he already knows, that he cannot, even if Congress were willing, sustain his promises of both free and adequately controlled use of such funds. The same thing may be said even of the "general sharing" money. If it is simply melded into the general funds of the benefited governments, as the Administration says it may be, how can its use be monitored and controlled unless total state or local expenditures are federally monitored? Mr. Nixon's briefers admitted that it's a valid question and wanly ducked it. All they could say about the problem was that a clause specifically including civil rights violations in the prohibitions connected with use of the money will be inserted in the draft legislation.

The first reactions in Congress suggested that such questions may be academic. Representative Wilbur Mills of Arkansas, Chairman of the Ways and Means Committee, and its ranking Republican member, John Byrnes of Wisconsin, declared their firm

opposition to essential aspects of Nixon revenue sharing. Mike
Mansfield of Montana, the Senate majority leader, indicated a
similar view in his gentler way. Unless the Administration gen-
erates a degree of support that its limited proposal last year signally
failed to arouse, the opposition of Mills and Byrnes alone will
doom revenue sharing. Federal reorganization on the scale proposed by Mr. Nixon was so remote a possibility that his White
House spokesmen expected no more than languid consideration of
it in 1971. If both proposals die, we shall see in 1972 whether
Mr. Nixon and his briefers are right in disclaiming any thought or
intention of settling for a good issue to run with in that Presidential
year.

February 6, 1971

——————

Not one of the major proposals discussed above and in subsequent
reports was enacted in 1971.

V

The Poor Betrayed

The White House staff was understandably anxious to have it believed that Mr. Nixon was not the man who made the decision announced on Saturday night, January 30, by Frank Carlucci, the director of the Office of Economic Opportunity, in the matter of California Rural Legal Assistance, Inc., a federally funded organization that provides the poor of rural California with legal aid which they cannot afford and have been denied in the past. The decision kept CRLA alive, but just barely, in circumstances and under conditions that could bring about its slow death. It was a wretched and dishonorable decision, the acknowledged result of a political deal with Governor Ronald Reagan, a decision that no decent man would want to be associated with. Unfortunately for the President, Governor Reagan made it impossible for him to escape association with it.

Reagan boasted in Sacramento, after a visit to Washington, that he had explained his objections to CRLA in a talk with the President at the White House on January 23, and said that he had received a sympathetic hearing. Subsequent events indicated that this was an understatement. Mr. Nixon was on holiday in the Virgin Islands when the decision was announced. All that his press spokesman, Ronald Ziegler, would say about it was that the President was informed of the decision before it was made public. Mr. Nixon's assistant for domestic affairs, John D. Ehrlichman, had a subordinate tell me for him on February 2 that he had not been involved—*"not at all,"* the subordinate emphasized—in the discussions between the White House staff and OEO officials that preceded the decision. The truth was that Ehrlichman took charge of the matter after Reagan had his talk with the President. Ehrlichman's instructions were to find a solution that would at least appear to keep CRLA alive and also would have the best possible political result. The best possible political result would have to be one that kept Governor Reagan happy and in a mood not to encourage Republicans around the country who would like to see him try in 1972, as he tried in 1968, to wrest the Presidential nomination from Richard Nixon. Finding such a solution took some doing. But it was done, thanks to Ehrlichman, as the simultaneous announcements issued on the 30th by Reagan and Frank Carlucci demonstrated.

Those announcements cannot be understood without a little background. Reagan has detested CRLA and its work for the California poor ever since it was founded in 1966, the year he was first elected governor. CRLA's 40-plus attorneys, mostly young and fired up for justice, have dared to bring into question and before the courts a variety of state, local and federal practices that deny poor Californians their elemental rights, and have won a high proportion of the cases. That is what OEO's 265 legal-service programs throughout the country are supposed to do. Some of them, CRLA included, do it with more vigor than others. CRLA's Chicano director, Cruz Reynoso, agrees that there have been excesses and some violations of OEO's strict guidelines, and several of the attorneys responsible for questioned behavior have left the program. But the OEO directorate in Washington has repeatedly cited CRLA to those in charge of other programs as *the* outstanding success, the one to be emulated elsewhere, and also as a program to be defended against the attacks to which it has been continually subjected.

One of its strongest defenders appeared until recently to be Donald Rumsfeld, the former OEO director who was transferred to the White House staff in December of 1970 and was succeeded by Frank Carlucci. Rumsfeld knew all there was to know about Reagan's hatred of the program and about the Governor's developing plan to veto any further federal funding of CRLA when, on December 1, OEO not only extended the California grant through 1971 but increased it by $205,539 to $1,884,101. Rumsfeld's announcement of the 1971 grant said that CRLA was "commonly recognized as one of the best Legal Services programs" and noted with pride that the National Legal Aid and Defender Association had declared it to be "the best such program" in 1968. Because of Reagan's known opposition and of the complaints regularly received from like-minded Californians, the CRLA operation had been examined with particular care by a team of OEO evaluators and later by an independent review committee that included former Supreme Court Justice Tom C. Clark. The OEO team and the Clark committee gave CRLA high marks and anyone might have thought that OEO and the Nixon White House were braced to stand firm against Reagan's clearly signalled intention to veto the 1971 grant.

Reagan vetoed it and the Administration instantly equivocated, extending the grant for only 30 days while professing to investigate no less than 127 charges brought against CRLA by the director of the state Office of Economic Opportunity, Lewis K. Uhler. One of the many odd aspects of the Uhler charges is that he, denouncing the use of public money to obstruct public actions, is paid from the OEO federal funds that support the state agency. I have read and reread every word of the remarkable Uhler document. Claiming no competence to judge it on my own, I defer to the opinion of a distinguished New York and Washington attorney, a man whose loyalty to the President is beyond question, who has read the Uhler report in line of duty and has said that it is unadulterated bunk. All of substance that it proves is that Governor Reagan and those who side with him in this affair are determined to see to it that federal money is not used in behalf of poor Americans in ways that discomfit well-off Americans and the federal, state and local government agencies that usually cater to their interests at the expense of poor Americans. A relevant fact is that

if the Reagan-Uhler charges were in the least justified, Frank
Carlucci and his White House mentors would be obligated to kill
CRLA and withhold any further federal funding at all. Carlucci
expressed his actual opinion of the Uhler report on the Thursday
before he announced his decision. At a meeting in Washington
with the lawyers who comprise OEO legal services' national ad-
visory committee, he said: "I sure as heck would hate to sustain a
veto on the basis of that report."

A way was found for him not only to sustain the Reagan veto
but to dignify the Uhler report in a fashion that was bound to do
immense harm to CRLA and to other OEO legal services programs. Carlucci, speaking the piece approved by Ehrlichman and
cleared with the President, announced that he had "reached an
agreement with Governor Reagan." The agreement provided that
Carlucci would "not override at this time Governor Reagan's
veto." Instead he made an entirely new grant (for $972,569), good
for six months and expiring July 31. In the meantime, he would
appoint a "high-level commission" to help him "complete a full
and impartial review of the matter." He would refer the Reagan-
Uhler report to the Justice Department and the Civil Service
Commission for check on "possible violations of federal law or
federal prohibitions on political activity" by CRLA employes.
And he would take the "fundamental policy questions raised by
the Governor's report" into consideration when he recommended
to Congress "new legislation dealing with the legal services program." The text of a gloating statement by Reagan was telephoned
from his Sacramento office to the OEO headquarters in Washington and was handed to CRLA representatives by an OEO official
within 30 minutes after they were given the Carlucci statement.
Reagan said he had "agreed with federal OEO to permit a short-
term extension of the grant for CRLA" and undertook to have a
state legal aid program ready "to take over legal assistance . . .
when the CRLA is phased out next July."

Carlucci's assistants, shaken by what one of them called "that
bastard's double-cross," rushed out an assertion that the six-month
extension "is not a phaseout or transition grant" and that CRLA
might yet be refunded in full for 1971. But the harm was done.
Reagan said on national TV that he expected other governors to
follow his example and veto objectionable legal services grants.
CRLA's headquarters officials in San Francisco, already struggling

with the staff and other difficulties brought upon them by the prolonged uncertainty, foresaw six months of distracting but unavoid-
able effort to counter the warning, implicit in the referrals to Justice
and the Civil Service Commission, that any poverty program lawyer
who did his job could be subject to federal penalties. It may have
constituted the best possible political result that John Ehrlichman
was assigned to bring about for the President. It was the worst
possible result for the nation's poor, a betrayal of them and the
cause of justice.

February 13, 1971

For CRLA's survival in better shape than I expected, see Chapter
XXI.

Games with Muskie

Mr. Nixon came up with a good environmental program on February 8. Russell E. Train, chairman of the Council on Environmental Quality and the President's ex-officio assistant in that field, over-spoke himself when he called it a great, truly remarkable and exciting program, loaded with "brand new" proposals and "a whole new set of new federal initiatives." But it was comprehensive, moderately bold by Nixon standards, a substantial extension of the 37 proposals for the control of pollution and preservation of the environment that the President submitted in a message to Congress in early 1970.

Perhaps the best testament to the 1971 Nixon program came in two ways from Senator Edmund S. Muskie of Maine. Senator Muskie, whose bid for the Presidency rests in part upon his standing as a dedicated protector of the environment, found nothing worth public criticism in the Nixon proposals when and immediately after they were announced in a second congressional message. He also flattered them by anticipation, including and enlarging upon several of them in a bill of his own that he introduced six days before Mr. Nixon sent up his message. In doing so, the Senator appeared to Russell Train and his associated environmental specialists to confirm their suspicion that the Muskie staff spends a good deal of its time and energies tracking prospective Administration moves in this policy area and seeing to it that Muskie gets there first with the most. It was this suspicion, embittered by Senator Muskie's current ascendancy over the President in public opinion polls, that accounted for and, in the view of Nixon people, justified the crass exclusion of Muskie from the White House ceremony at which the President signed and took credit for an air pollution bill that the Senator had strengthened and guided to enactment. Nixon assistants argued at the time that they merely played tit for tat on that occasion. They felt that the press, in making a martyr of the snubbed Senator, should have noted that he is not above environmental scene stealing.

Senator Muskie said the other day in another connection (Indochina policy) that he does not let his budding rivalry with the President influence his views on serious questions. Muskie assistants naturally maintain that line, but they do not take it to the point of denying that the Senator and the President do a certain amount of environmental cribbing from each other. They say pretty much what is heard at the White House—namely, that in a policy field as thoroughly ploughed as the environment has been, there are no really new ideas and no claimants to exclusive possession of the available ideas. To an extent that must vex the Nixon people when they think about it, and offers the Muskie people large opportunities for future exploitation, the same observation applies to several other policy areas now in favour with the President. Between 1962 and 1969, when Mr. Nixon was climbing from the abyss to the Presidency, Senator Muskie was making a record for himself, surprising in its breadth to anyone who hitherto has overlooked it, in such matters as the sharing of federal revenues with states and localities, bringing structured order into federal-state relationships, draft reform, and improvement of the President's own administrative and policy mechanisms.

The subject of the Muskie-Nixon contest for preeminence in environmental protection is handled with mingled frankness and delicacy by the Senator's assistants. "The Senator feels," one of

'DICK, ARE YOU HAVING THOSE DREAMS AGAIN?'

them said just before Mr. Nixon sent his latest program to Congress, "that you preempt by performance and not by rhetoric. So I don't think the Senator really worries much about whether the President is doing any preempting." Another Muskie assistant addressed himself to the question of preemption as it is posed at the White House. "I can see why they might be a little sensitive on this," the Muskie man said. "It's always been the Senator's practice to accept good ideas, whatever the origin."

Reporters trying to get some advance indication of the President's 1971 program noticed in late 1970 that Russell Train and others who were shaping up the program were more anxious to keep the details from Muskie than from the public. It was a vain endeavor. The Muskie staff knew what to expect in the Nixon message well before it was either submitted or cleared with the Republican leadership in Congress and before, incidentally, Muskie's previously mentioned "Water Quality Standards Act of 1971" was introduced on February 2. Train told reporters on February 8 that they would have to await delivery to Congress of 14 bills implementing the Nixon proposals. Leon Billings, a Muskie man on the Senate Public Works Committee staff, had in hand that day the 20 original Administration drafts from which the 14 bills to be submitted were still being condensed. It has appeared to Muskie's staff for many months that their communication with federal agencies and departments has been steadily constricted, either at White House instruction or simply from the natural caution of a highly politicized bureaucracy. But in vital matters, such as forthcoming Nixon proposals that particularly interest Muskie, the intelligence service continues to function. "We still have some friends down there," a Muskie man said, meaning at the White House and in its vicinity.

Nixon proposed to increase federal grants for municipal sewage treatment from the present $1.25 billion to $2 billion a year, with a total of $6 billion over three years. Muskie's bill upped the ante to $2.5 billion a year, for five years, and with provision for matching funds aimed at an overall $25 billion sewage program instead of Nixon's $12 billion. Muskie similarly proposed, just ahead of Nixon, the strengthening of federal water-quality standards, their extension to navigable and other waters not now covered; and broadened requirements that the standards be applied to industrial and other private sources of pollution. A proposal prized by Nixon would empower the new Environmental Protection Agency to restrict and penalize the production and use of toxic chemicals and metals that may contaminate the waters. Muskie dealt with that one, too. The Senator's men could claim, and did, that he had been years ahead of Nixon with controls on ocean dumping and proposals that utilities be required to preplan, in stages of from two to ten years, the siting and construction of power plants and power lines, so that state governments and, if necessary, the federal government could curb adverse environmental effects.

The one proposal that put Nixon ahead of Muskie was to penalize, with a special tax, both the production and use of high-sulphur coal and fuel oil. Whether to place the major emphasis at points of production or at points of use was still to be decided, in consultation with the same House Ways and Means and Senate Finance committees that refused last year to consider and report for passage a similar Nixon tax on high-lead gasolines.

Muskie could claim only peripheral pioneering of what the President labelled a new national land-use policy. The national policy appeared to consist principally of encouraging state governments to adopt and enforce adequate land policies and, in the process, to take over from local governments many of their present zoning and other restrictive powers. Muskie has long contended that sufficient guidance and control of land use at state and local levels can be accomplished only when the wide variations in property taxation are rationalized and standardized. The Nixon message omitted any reference to national land standards that the states might be required to meet. Train and Rogers Morton, the new Secretary of the Interior, seemed at a White House briefing on the message to evade questions about that omission, as if the Administration did not want at this stage to deal with factors that might becloud its contention that the way to improve state performance in this and many other policy areas is to put maximum responsibility and minimum federal control upon state governments. This approach is basic to Nixon's emerging philosophy of government. Whatever they may think of it, liberal critics of the Administration will have to recognize it as a serious Nixon objective and a serious challenge to the liberal assumption that state governments are inherently deficient.

February 20, 1971

———

Nixon lobbyists did their utmost to prevent enactment of a Muskie bill that transferred much of the responsibility for anti-pollution enforcement from the states to the federal government and imposed harsher penalties—with earlier deadlines for compliance—than the President thought either necessary or practicable.

VII

To Your Health

The architects of Mr. Nixon's "national health strategy" understood from the start of their work on it that he expected them to justify and act upon the view, which he stated and italicized in his message to Congress on February 18, that "there is much that is *right* with American medicine." He acknowledged in the next sentence that "there is also much that is wrong," but he didn't give the word "wrong" comparable emphasis. Richard Nathan, an assistant director of the Office of Management and Budget, adhered to that relative estimate of what is right and what is wrong with the present system (or nonsystem) of health care when he drafted, for the President, the original report from which he and other White House assistants and technicians at the Department of Health, Education, and Welfare evolved the Nixon program. During the months of preparatory debate and discussion, including intermittent consultation with the President, the officials shaping up the program never deviated from or considered any major alternative to Mr. Nixon's basic proposition that the existent structure of private practice supported mainly by private means and commercial insurance was to be built upon rather than discarded or fundamentally altered. The guiding rule was the one set forth in the President's message: "While it would be wrong to ignore any weaknesses in our present system, it would be equally wrong to sacrifice its strengths."

Mr. Nixon placed his program in competition with two principal alternatives. One of them is embodied in a bill sponsored by Edward Kennedy and 24 other senators and by Representative Martha Griffiths and more than 100 co-signers in the House. The other, resembling the Nixon approach in its philosophy, is the American Medical Association's "Medicredit" plan. Several others (the AMA listed a total of eight in a February study) are also before Congress. But the Nixon, Kennedy and AMA programs are the ones from which legislation is likely to be developed, and the least to be said for the President is that in presenting his own proposals he made it all but certain that this session of Congress will face up in a serious way to the need for something that deserves to be called a national health system. Senator Kennedy, critical though he was of the Nixon plan, credited the Administration with promoting a needed "national dialogue" in and outside Congress. Senator Abraham Ribicoff of Connecticut, whose concern with the health problem predates Senator Kennedy's, similarly praised the President in the course of announcing that he is devising his own alternative to the Nixon, Kennedy and AMA programs.

The Nixon White House has a habit of throwing out its grand designs, in the form of Presidential messages, weeks and sometimes months ahead of the draft legislation that contains the actual substance. A week after the President's seemingly comprehensive health message was published, his and HEW Secretary Elliot Richardson's assistants were still sweating out the legislation to be considered by congressional committees. Even with the Administration drafts in hand, the committees will have to fill in some sizable holes in the Nixon message. The committees may be confronted with a final program that is stronger in some respects and weaker in others than the outline offered in the message appears to be.

The Nixon scheme deals separately with Americans who can afford to pay for their health care and with those who cannot. But it deals with the poor and the nonpoor in the same way—by reliance

'GET AWAY FROM ME WITH THAT FILTHY STUFF – YOU...SOCIALIST!!'

upon privately provided health insurance. The federal government would buy the insurance for families with no or very low incomes (up to $3000 for a family of four). An official fact sheet supplementing the Nixon message said that "all employers of one or more persons" would be required by law to provide "minimum standard health insurance protection" for their employes, with the employers paying at least 65 percent of the cost initially and 75 percent later on. The employes would pay the rest, unless they or their unions obtained higher or total employer payment. The fine print limited the superficially inclusive mandate to employers "engaged in interstate commerce," a very broad but not totally embracing category.

The "minimum protection" to be required was not defined, leaving the impression that it could, with one generous exception, consist of the cheapest and most limited coverage available through Blue Cross and similar private insurance arrangements. The exception, insisted upon by the President, was the provision of coverage up to $50,000 for catastrophic illness of the kind that took the life of a tubercular older brother and burdened the Nixon family in Mr. Nixon's boyhood. Covered employes would get full maternity care and preventive care for children, but they would have to pay the first $100 to $208 of hospital costs and a vaguely indicated proportion of medical costs. The very poor would not have to meet these costs, but families of four with incomes above $3000 would have to pay some of the costs and, at income levels above $5000, all of them. Secretary Richardson guessed that employers in the first year would have to pay $7 billion a year more than employers now pay for health insurance. But he conceded that this and literally all other cost estimates, for the Nixon and rival programs, are no better than guesses and flimsy guesses at that. The only thing he seemed to be reasonably sure of was that the added federal cost would be in the range of $3 billion the first year, rising afterward but never to the level of cost to the federal treasury required by the Kennedy approach.

It can be argued, as Kennedy and his cohorts do, that cost considerations should not obscure the profound significance of his proposal that the present structure of private and commercial health insurance be discarded and replaced by truly national and federalized insurance, underwriting what in effect would come close to being a nationalized health service. It would be nationalized and federalized in the sense that nearly all doctors, their nondegree assistants, hospitals and other health-care institutions would get most of their money from the federal government rather than from patients and insurance companies. Medical and associated practitioners would be subject to compulsions, direct and indirect, much stronger and likely to be more effective than any proposed or implied in the Nixon and AMA programs. But federal cost is a factor that is sure to influence the choices that Congress makes, and the Kennedy proponents have been less than frank in their cost projections. The total Kennedy first-year cost is likely to be nearer the $80 billion predicted by Secretary Richardson than to the $41 billion (based on 1969 experience) that the Kennedy people bandy about. Half of it—probably $35 to $40 billion—would come from the federal government's general revenues, and it would require the addition of somewhere between $20–$30 billion to the sums presently budgeted for health purposes. The other half would come from employers and employes, through payroll taxes superimposed upon present Social Security taxes. In return, the covered beneficiaries, taxpayers and the whole society would have a genuinely inclusive national health care system, guaranteeing to everyone the total costs of most but not all necessary care. Nursing-home and psychiatric care would be severely restricted, for instance. AMA's Medicredit, offering minimal coverage at federal expense to people who pay no income taxes and equivalent coverage at ascending cost to those who do pay income taxes, does not begin to meet the need on the Kennedy scale.

All three proposals pretend to deal with the related problems of the supply of medical care and of the inflated and still inflating charges for that care. But none of the three, the Kennedy approach included, really meets these problems in a convincing way. The Kennedy plan, for example, relies upon the prior allocation of fixed sums to designated localities and areas, on the assumption that doctors, technicians and institutions will hold total charges within the promised total of payment. Nixon relies upon "competition" and upon the promotion of prepaid group care ("Health Maintenance Organizations") to hold down charges. Financial incentives, considerably stronger in the Kennedy plan than in the Nixon plan, are expected to increase medical school enrollments and induce doctors and other medical professionals to provide needed services in the ghetto and rural areas that are presently unserved or under-served. All of the major proposals—Nixon, Kennedy, AMA—shy away from the kind and degree of control and compulsion that nobody wants and that the problem may require.

March 6, 1971

———

National health insurance remained to be enacted, and the issues remained pretty much as defined above, in early 1972.

VIII

Black Study

The members of Congress who comprise the Black Caucus in the House of Representatives have never acknowledged their debt to the Reverend Ralph David Abernathy. They largely owe to him the favor the President did them by refusing for a year to receive them in a group at the White House. Mr. Nixon's traumatic reaction to their bid for recognition would not have become the study in Administration attitudes that it did become if Ralph Abernathy had behaved with the decorum that is expected of White House visitors after he had a session with the President and his Cabinet on May 13, 1969. Nixon appeared to close the Caucus episode with friendly grace when he said at his February 17 press conference that he thought a meeting with the black members was going to be worked out and added, "I hope it is, because I will be glad to talk to them, of course." But the whole of his answer to a question about the affair was actually a further study in non-comprehension, a fitting climax to the prolonged failure at the White

House to understand the people and the problem that Mr. Nixon and his assistants were dealing with.

The encounter with the Reverend Abernathy was arranged by Daniel P. Moynihan, then in the bloom of his reputation as the Nixon assistant who understood black people better than black people understood themselves. Abernathy, who was trying to prove himself a worthy successor to Martin Luther King at the head of the Southern Christian Leadership Conference, was in Washington with a troop of followers, galumphing from department to department with a set of "demands" that, upon examination, turned out to be pretty much in line with the promises Mr. Nixon was already making to better the lot of black Americans. Moynihan calculated that an invitation to the White House, for a talk with the President and his Cabinet Council on Urban Affairs, would at once cool down Abernathy and show the President's good faith. It seemed to Moynihan and other assistants at the meeting that it worked that way. The President, they said afterward, was in top form and Abernathy at the Cabinet table was suitably respectful and grateful. If he was, the Reverend Abernathy underwent a drastic change during his short walk from the Cabinet Room to the White House lawn, where the press awaited him. He bellowed into radio and television microphones that his session with the President and Cabinet had been "the most disappointing and the most pointless of all the meetings we have had up to this time." Moynihan, standing by, choked with rage. One of his assistants was heard to exclaim, "Why, the son of a bitch!" Many months afterward, Mr. Nixon was said to have felt and still to feel that the performance was not so much a personal affront as an offense against the Presidency, a lesson to him that he must never again offer the White House as a platform to people who might abuse it as he thought Ralph Abernathy had done. Certainly the effects were lasting. The memory figured specifically and importantly in the Nixon staff's dealings with the Black Caucus, once the staff got around to what passed for dealings with it.

Happily for the Caucus and its cause, that took a long time. Variously ignored and rebuffed as it was for months, a request that would have led at most to a bit of transient drama was allowed to grow into a symbolic issue between the President and black Americans. The originator of the notion that black members of Congress have a special right of access to the President and that he has a special duty to grant it was William L. (Bill) Clay, a sometime real estate and insurance man who in February of 1970 was a first-term congressman from St. Louis. There then were nine black House members. All of them were Democrats. All but one of them, the aging and now dead William Dawson of Chicago, voted a consistently liberal and frequently anti-Administration line. But they were not demagogues, not a particularly fearsome lot. Viewed in the total House perspective, they were rather tame. They were not in fact the cohesive band that Bill Clay made them out to be when he drafted and, on February 18 of 1970, sent to the President a letter asking him to meet with the nine. The White House has not released the letter and Clay has misplaced his only copy of it. It was said to be a brief and courteous note, requesting (as Clay later put it) a meeting "to discuss a range of questions representing the concerns of 25 million black Americans." Given no answer, Clay twice telephoned the White House. Robert Brown, the only black assistant on the President's immediate staff, and Herbert Klein, the Director of Communications, counselled patience and said the letter would be brought to the President's attention. The sole evidence that Nixon had seen it came on April 20. Hugh W. Sloan, Jr., a very subordinate staff assistant, wrote Clay that "we had hoped to be able to work this out . . . but we just have not been able to work it in." Clay took this to be the rebuff it was and said on the House floor that "the members of the Black Caucus . . . make known at this time our outright disgust with the President's policies and his refusal to give us an audience."

Clay and two colleagues, Augustus F. Hawkins of California and Louis Stokes of Ohio, sent the President a second letter on July 23. It was rough, barely courteous, to the point ("you have traveled to all corners of the earth . . . but you have not come to black America"). It quoted and deplored the explanation of the April rebuff that John Ehrlichman, the President's assistant for domestic affairs, had given *Time:* "We try not to permit opportunists to use the Presidency as a grandstand." William E. Timmons, a staff lobbyist who is responsible for relationships with the House, wrote Clay on July 27 that "your letter will be brought to the President's attention."

The blacks were otherwise ignored until September when one

of them, John Conyers of Michigan, telephoned Leonard Garment, a Nixon assistant who has a better feel for racial niceties than most of his associates. The only result of several Conyers-Garment conversations was confusion. Garment recalled the Abernathy business, said a repetition of it would harm the blacks and offend the President, and argued for a discussion that would go to general attitudes and issues rather than to disputed specifics. He thought that Conyers agreed. Conyers' black colleagues got an impression from him that Garment was implying, if not laying down, conditions that they considered insulting. Congressman Clark Mac-Gregor of Minnesota, who had been defeated for the Senate in the November elections and was about to join Nixon as his lobbyist-in-chief, next entered the picture, again in conversation with Conyers, and more confusion resulted. The word got around that MacGregor had said that the President was ready to meet the blacks in December and Conyers had told MacGregor that it would be better to wait until five new black members took their seats in the 92nd Congress. This was embarrassing to the blacks because, if the story of the Conyers-MacGregor conversation was true, it made their trumpeted boycott of the President's State of the Union address in January even cruder and more futile than it then appeared to many people (this writer included) to be. It was not true, according to Conyers and to Ronald Ziegler, the President's press secretary. Unfortunately for Senator Edward Brooke, the black Republican from Massachusetts, he thought it was true and said so after the boycott occurred and the President, suddenly bestirring himself, asked Brooke to be his intermediary.

"I talked to Senator Brooke about that just a few days ago," Mr. Nixon said on February 17, "and asked him to speak to some of those who had made this request." This remark, made in good spirit by the President, betrayed the insensitivity that had attended his and his staff's entire conduct of the affair. Brooke was embarrassed by the President's request, though he complied with it. He understood that the black representatives resented what they regarded as a gratuitous intrusion. Brooke's version of the Mac-Gregor-Conyers discussion infuriated them. Some of them said, with profane emphasis, that the President or any one of his assistants could have called any one of them at any time and arranged a meeting. It looks at this writing as if the meeting that could have

occurred in 1970 will occur soon, with no credit to the President
and minimal satisfaction to the Black Caucus.

March 13, 1971

———

The meeting occurred in late March and was not repeated in 1971.

IX

Selling
the "Revolution"

Mr. Nixon's effort to sell his "new American revolution" since he proclaimed it in his State of the Union message suggests that he really believes that it can be "as profound, as far-reaching, as exciting as that first revolution almost 200 years ago." The thought that Tricky Dick is at it again, inviting the Democratic majorities in Congress to reject his main proposals and thereby give him a winning issue in 1972, simply does not match up with the elaborate campaign to generate support that the President is waging, partly in person and partly with the commanded help of his Cabinet Secretaries, their chief assistants, his own assistants at the White House, and the reorganized leadership and staff of the Republican National Committee. Cooperative governors (Nelson Rockefeller notably among them), mayors, county officials, state legislators, the heads and paid executives of business and professional and governmental associations have been addressed, lobbied, briefed, deluged with White House mail. The Vice President has been directed to forego the headlines that gaudier endeavors earn him and devote himself to prosaic but necessary arguments for Nixon revenue-sharing. The President has invited every member of Congress to the White House for breakfast meetings, smaller huddles and individual sessions. Selling the revolution has been made the first business of his domestic assistants, high and low. They have been instructed to pass up no opportunities that come their way, and to seek others, to get out of their offices and preach the revolution.

The priorities established for this massive effort are informative. Welfare reform, which the President called "the most important" of all his programs in his January message, gets no more than incidental attention, perhaps because the critical fight for it is going on within the House Ways and Means Committee. Draft reform, his environmental program and his proposal for limited national health insurance figure in the promotional briefings and speeches. So, with somewhat greater emphasis, does the proposal to merge seven domestic departments into four consolidated monsters. But the Nixon measure that gets the big push is revenue sharing, the two-part program that the President in Des Moines termed his "$16 billion investment in renewing state and local government."

This is interesting, for several reasons. The priority reflects Mr. Nixon's familiar fascination with government and its processes, with the problems of making it work as he thinks it should. However engrossing and attractive the prospect of sharing federal revenues may be, at least in principle, to incumbent state and local officials, it is not an inherently popular and appealing issue. The sluggish response of senators and representatives in both parties to it cannot have surprised Mr. Nixon. He can hardly think that in revenue sharing, win or lose in Congress, he has an issue that will importantly affect the national elections next year. Yet he puts it at the top of his revolutionary agenda and acts as if he is determined to keep it there. Why? Shared revenue entails shared responsibility—not as much sharing of responsibility as the President and his spokesmen appear to claim but do not actually claim; but certainly enough to make some of the difference in the federal system that he says it will make. One has to believe, observing the President's commitment to his proposition, that he has the confidence in state and local government that he professes to have and that he believes the difference will be enough to "give the people of America a chance, a bigger voice in deciding for themselves those questions that so greatly affect their lives."

The burden of sustaining the President's proposition that state and local governments are closer and more responsive to "the people" than the federal government is falls, not upon him, but upon the officials who have to draft and expound his legislation. They have found that it is much easier to talk about shucking federal responsibility than it is to shuck responsibility. "General" revenue sharing provides a good example of the difficulty. This is the form of sharing that in principle promises states and localities $5 billion in the first operative year, rising to $10 billion a year by 1980, in federal tax money they can spend as they please. But, it turns out, not altogether as they please. The recipients must tell the Secretary of the Treasury what they propose to use the money for. Discriminatory denial of its benefits to any citizen "on the ground of race, color or national origin" is forbidden and punishable. The governor of each state is to be the Treasury's enforcement agent, and there is plenty of room for governors to protect their friends in local and county governments. But in the end the local officials and the governors are liable to penalties ranging from cut-off of further federal founds to civil suit to recover misused funds. Their budgets are subject to federal audit, a feature of the proposal that the President minimizes and his spokesmen are extremely reluctant to discuss. It takes the sheen off the promise of free funds to be freely used by the receiving governments without federal supervision.

The companion "special" revenue sharing is shot through with similar and greater anomalies. This is the form of sharing that lumps 130 federal grant programs into six general-purpose programs and is supposed to simplify the distribution to states and localities of $11.4 billion a year for urban and rural development, law enforcement, education, manpower training, and transportation. The simplest of these, the one intended to give states and localities the utmost discretion in their use of the federal money, is for law enforcement. Mr. Nixon introduced Attorney General Mitchell when he appeared in the White House press room to explain its virtues. Mitchell had a terrible time with the provision that state and local governments must submit comprehensive plans but don't have to get federal approval of the plans. What then, he was asked, did the federal government require? "In the last analysis," Mitchell answered, "it is a requirement that they (the recipients) comply with their own plan." He was reminded that the Justice Department recently had to step in and correct the scandalous misuse of law-enforcement grants in Alabama, and was asked what he could and would do in such a situation if the new system is adopted. "I don't think we need get into what might have been or will be until the actual circumstances are presented to us," he replied.

George Romney, the Secretary of Housing and Urban Development, made a convincing case at his press briefing that the proposed substitution of shared revenues for restricted grants will ease and simplify both the distribution and the use of federal funds for community development. But he, too, had to acknowledge that the vaunted freedom being offered state and local governments isn't all that complete. What if a mayor and city council used federal money to replace a neighborhood with a football stadium and called it community development? "They can't just do anything with community development funds," Romney answered. "They will know that if they want more money through the discretionary funds, they had better do a good job because otherwise they won't get some additional funds from that source."

John Ehrlichman, the President's assistant for domestic affairs, preferred in his numerous briefings to minimize federal compulsion and emphasize the corrective power of state and local electorates. Ehrlichman was the busiest and probably the most effective of the President's briefers, in all but continuous meetings with congressmen, businessmen, editors, working newsmen. He showed himself to be knowledgeable, frank within limits, a true believer. He also gave some examples of the quality of talk heard at the Nixon White House, from its very best performers. "If people are getting mugged on every street corner and the police cars don't operate," Ehrlichman said the other day, "and the city council meets and instead of putting additional money into law enforcement they go for a tax reduction, I think you could see where that eventually would lead in terms of local realities." At the same briefing: "If the county supervisors decide that three statues will be erected in the county to their respective wives, made of Italian marble. . . . I think that is something that could be put into the political process of the locality by simply airing that intention."

March 20, 1971

X

Kissinger and Rogers

After saying at a press conference on March 4 that Secretary of State William P. Rogers is "the foreign policy adviser for the President" and "the chief foreign policy spokesman for the President," Mr. Nixon continued: "Now, the role of Dr. Kissinger is a different one. He is the White House adviser to the President. He covers not only foreign policy but national security policy, the coordination of those policies." That was a sufficient and convincing answer to the question to which the President was addressing himself. The question, as he stated it a moment later, was "whether either Secretary Rogers or Dr. Kissinger is the top adviser," and the answer implicit in what Mr. Nixon had said was that Henry A. Kissinger is "the top adviser." But the President didn't leave it at that. He felt that he had to repeat himself and say that the answer to the question as he had phrased it "is very simply that the Secretary of State is always the chief foreign policy adviser and the chief foreign policy spokesman of the Administration."

It was a sensitive question for the President, one that had been rubbing him raw since early February. His reaction then to a casual and generally overlooked statement by George D. Aiken, the dean of Republican Senators, showed when it became known that Mr. Nixon was beginning to realize that his prized system of foreign and national security policy development had seriously impaired the position and effectiveness of Secretary Rogers. A brief news item quoted Aiken's remark that Rogers did not seem to be involved in major foreign policy decisions. Mr. Nixon immediately wrote a letter to the senator, assuring him that Rogers was involved in all major foreign policy decisions. Aiken said nothing about the letter until March 2, when a Nixon assistant startled him by asking him not only to release it but to publicize it at a press conference. Senator Aiken declined to call a press conference, but he agreed to answer any questions that he might be asked about the letter and to have it printed in the *Congressional Record*.

The request to Aiken was one of several White House responses, capped by the President's remarks on March 4, to the complaints of two other senators that Henry Kissinger had damagingly overshadowed Rogers and, what was worse, had done it in a fashion that denied Congress as a whole and the Senate Foreign Relations Committee in particular their proper roles in the evolution and execution of foreign policy. The committee chairman, Senator Fulbright, and one of its members, Stuart Symington, raised the old and tattered issue of "executive privilege." They said that Kissinger, by invoking it and refusing to submit to committee questioning, had frustrated them and their colleagues in their right and efforts to get at the real origins and intent of Nixon policy. Symington, graphically detailing the structure of departmental committees, groups and staff processes that Kissinger devised and directs, said that the President's assistant for national security affairs is "the most powerful man in the Nixon Administration next to the President himself" and asserted that his immunity from committee interrogation "nullifies the basic concept of advice and consent." Fulbright drafted a bill that would require Kissinger and other Presidential assistants to appear upon command before the Foreign Relations and other committees, if only to say that they had been specifically directed in writing by the President to refuse to testify. It was a feeble threat, likely to die in Fulbright's committee, and the President would probably have ridden out the furor in silence if Kissinger's ascendancy had not been related to what Symington called "a resultant obvious decline in the prestige and position of the Secretary of State and his department."

Symington also said in a Senate speech, "Wherever one goes in the afternoon or evening around this town, one hears our very able Secretary of State laughed at. People say he is Secretary of State in title only." That did it. A White House assistant forthwith got in touch with Senator Aiken, as noted. Mr. Nixon ordered his press secretary, Ronald Ziegler, to tell reporters that "President Nixon has the utmost confidence in the Secretary of State" and that "those who may have the impression that the Secretary of State is not the President's chief adviser on foreign affairs are misleading themselves and others." The staff of *Monday,* a weekly propaganda sheet put out by the Republican National Committee, polled two Washington society columnists and four "prominent Washington hostesses" and reported their "unanimous" testimony that "they had never heard the Secretary of State laughed at."

Mr. Nixon made the difficulty for himself and for his Secretary of State when he fulfilled his 1968 campaign pledge "to restore the National Security Council to its preeminent role in national security planning." Henry Kissinger's preeminence, his own skills apart, is a product of that promised and accomplished preeminence. Symington recognized this when he maintained, on the Senate floor and personally to Rogers, that he was aiming at neither Rogers nor Kissinger but at "the concentration of foreign policy decision-making power in the White House" and at the isolation of that power center from Congress. Senator Jacob Javits, agreeing with Symington that "excessive use of executive privilege" had impeded congressional oversight of foreign policy, went to the core of the matter when he asked, "Why should we not hold the President himself responsible rather than Dr. Kissinger for the effect upon Congress of the organization of his Presidency respecting international security affairs?" Mr. Nixon, reacting in behalf of his "oldest and closest friend in the Cabinet," the Secretary of State, acknowledged the responsibility for the concentration and did what he could to offset the result that he, with Kissinger as his instrument, had brought about.

Kissinger took it all with a great show of calm. He and the President had just come to an understanding that he, Kissinger,

was welcome to remain at the White House as long as he pleased
and to leave when he chose. The President sealed the understanding on January 16 with an extraordinary letter in which he said
to Kissinger, "Frankly, I cannot imagine what the government
would be like without you . . . I am grateful for what you have
done and I am grateful that you are staying." Kissinger perceived
that he was only an incidental target of the Symingtons and
Fulbrights. His concern, it was said at the White House, was not
for himself but for the NSC and interdepartmental policy structure
that serves the President through him. He believes, as the President
does, that it is a necessary response to the pressures and requirements of the times and that, if retained, it can be a permanent
asset to the Presidency.

Two years after Kissinger began putting the structure together
for the President, it still defies precise description. The NSC staff
at its top and center consists at this writing of 42 professional
foreign service officers, coordinators, policy and program analysts.
A web of interdepartmental groups and committees at the levels
of assistant secretaries and under secretaries channels the President's requirements to the departments through Kissinger and,
also through him, draws the information and judgments of the
concerned departments and agencies into the White House for
final appraisal and decision. Kissinger is chairman of the most
important panels, groups and committees, and a Kissinger man
sits on each of the others. He dominates the entire process up to
the point where, at NSC meetings and in the Oval Office, the
product reaches the President. Then the President dominates, a
fact that tends to be overlooked by those who fret over such
questions as whether Rogers or Kissinger has the last and decisive
word with the President.

The second year of the Kissinger reign brought some changes.
In his NSC shop, there is less emphasis than there was at first upon
long-term policy planning and thinking by his own people and
more upon extracting plans and thinking of the desired quality
from State, Defense, the Joint Chiefs, CIA. Kissinger is increasing
his budget for outside consultants from $132,000 to $458,000.
The NSC staff's review, criticism and supplementation of the papers that flow to the White House is, if anything, more rigorous

than ever. Many of the directives that go out to the departments and agencies seem at the receiving end to be more detailed, more explicit in the questions raised and the criteria set for response to the questions than they used to be. Intent to predetermine the answers is denied at the White House, but that seems to some of the recipients, particularly at the State Department, to be the effect. Even the complainers grant, however, that Kissinger is wholly impartial when he presents varying views to the Council and to the President. It is said for him, and people who work with him say it is true, that he saves his own views for the President and never knowingly tries to swing the preparatory process one way or another.

Although friction between the NSC staff and State has lessened, contrary reports notwithstanding, Kissinger's dealings with foreign ambassadors continue to be a source of resentment at the department and of some embarrassment to him. A department spokesman's recent statement that Kissinger's ventures in direct diplomacy had led to an "understanding" between State and the White House irritated him. He felt that it was a subject best left in limbo. The story at the White House is that Kissinger traffics with ambassadors only in instances of extreme need, at the instructions of the President and with a few ambassadors who demand contact with him as evidence that the President cherishes their principals at home.

Working for him is hell, now as before, but he has tried in the last year or so to make it less hellish than it was at first. He knows that he lost some good men because he excluded them from him. Now his senior assistants see him at least once on most days, and the juniors hear through their own superiors when he likes their work. But the tensions within the staff are still enormous and unrelenting. This is partly because of the sheer work pressure, partly because Kissinger deliberately sets one staffer against another on the same assignments, usually without telling them that he has. He tells them now what they once had to guess: that one of their principal uses is to replenish his own store of knowledge and judgment, a store that he thought inexhaustible when he came to the White House but now finds to have been drained and diminished by the demands of the first two years. His readiness to admit as much, and to joke with his people about his driving and sometimes cruel ways, is said by the driven to be one of his appealing qualities, among the qualities that make it a rewarding hell.

The fact is that Henry the curmudgeon can be a nicer and more kindly fellow than he wants to be told by the people who work for him. "Working for Henry," an assistant remarked the other day, "you learn never to say to him, 'Thank you, Henry.' He doesn't like it; it embarrasses him. He does lots of things, little personal things, that you want to thank him for, but you don't do it if you know what's good for you." There isn't much time for thanking Henry, in any case. K. Wayne Smith, the chief of Kissinger's program analysts, hasn't taken a day completely off in nine months. He and others in his situation are bound to get jaded, and they do. It's one of several aspects of the Kissinger operation that justify a certain doubt. One of the doubts is whether it is or can be the permanent contribution to government that Kissinger and the President think it should be. A structure and a process so thoroughly dominated by and dependent upon Henry Kissinger is likely to be no more permanent than his tenure at the White House. Maybe the President knew this when he wrote that letter to Kissinger in January.

March 27, 1971

———

My reference to Kissinger's "sometimes cruel ways" distressed him, and I noted later that the word "cruel" was poorly chosen.

XI

More about Kissinger

My last report on the roles of Secretary of State William P. Rogers and the President's adviser, Henry Kissinger, left unsaid a good deal that seems worth saying about Kissinger. Here, then, are some additional impressions and thoughts.

Kissinger's recently disclosed habit of meeting at the White House with opponents of the Indochina war is in character with him and with his conception of the job that the President excepts him to do. Eugene McCarthy lunched with Kissinger in his elegant White House office on March 15. Senator George McGovern had breakfast with him there on March 12. A Catholic nun, a Quaker professor of physics and a young antiwar activist, all of them named by the Justice Department as co-conspirators in the alleged plot of the Berrigan brothers to kidnap Kissinger, met with him in the basement war-room at the White House on March 6. Kissinger has had four talks in the past 12 months with Averell Harriman and two with Harriman's former deputy at the abortive Paris peace negotiations, Cyrus Vance. Twenty-one other meetings with prominent individual critics of Nixon war policy have included four with John Kenneth Galbraith, two with John Gardner of Common Cause. There have been 19 meetings with groups of antiwar students, 28 with delegations of antiwar professors and teachers, 56 with other academic groups that didn't come to protest but included critics of Nixon policy.

Why Kissinger does it and what he and the President hope to get out of it are good questions. One is told and must believe that Nixon and his adviser are not fools enough to suppose that a chat with Henry Kissinger will alter the views of Gene McCarthy or George McGovern. Kissinger is not about to give his critics a chance to go from his office to the camera and say that he tried and failed to convert them. Politics enters, of course: anything that tends to quiet protest and to evince a readiness to hear out the critics is to the President's political advantage. McGovern got a distinct impression that Kissinger would have been disappointed if their meeting had remained the secret that Kissinger later said he wanted and intended it to be. Although Kissinger is outraged by the suggestion that his meetings with professors and the like may also be to his advantage, to the extent that they moderate hostility toward him in the academic community, he would be less than human if the thought didn't cross his mind.

But I prefer another answer, derived from the answers heard at the White House. It is that the many hours taken from Kissinger's crowded schedule for such meetings reflect his desire and the President's to diminish the damage that both of them know the Indochina war and Nixon war policy are doing to American society. Kissinger speaks of the need for "a reconciliation of society" in terms and in a manner that allow no doubt of his conviction that it must be accomplished and that the war will prove to be a greater national tragedy than it already is if the reconciliation that he tries to prepare and further with his meetings is not accomplished.

Kissinger's sense of the need and the tragedy does not inspire him to welcome or advocate an end of the war on the terms that the critics whom he invites to the White House advocate. Some of them recognize and grant, however, that Kissinger in his sessions with the critics is attempting in his fashion to serve a purpose larger than the immediate interests of the Administration. The attempt seems comical to some, ironical or futile to others. It

'FIRST OF ALL I WANT YOU TO ISSUE A STATEMENT DENYING IT ....'

interests me because it tells things about Henry Kissinger that otherwise might not be apparent. Tom Davidson, one of the Berrigan three, remarked to columnist Mary McGrory after their meeting with Kissinger that "he's got this weird thing for us who operate out of the morality bag; he sees himself as the conscience of the Administration." Doubtful though Senator McGovern was that his meeting was of any use, he said that the unspoken question that appeared to pervade his discussion with Kissinger was, "How do we resolve this thing with minimum disruption of our society?" Minimum disruption could connote minimum opposition to the war, but McGovern did not recall that Kissinger sought either to minimize or to decry opposition. It was conceivable though not at the time apparent to him, McGovern said after some reflection, that raising the problem of disruption and encouraging future thought about it was Kissinger's principal purpose in inviting him to the White House.

In his conversations with invited dissidents, at his famous background briefings for the press, and in private talks with reporters and commentators, Kissinger takes the greatest care to conceal any differences that may exist between him and the President and, indeed, between him and such other participants in the foreign policy and national security process as the Secretaries of State and Defense. The only policies that he discusses and (invariably) defends are the President's declared policies. A result is that trying to identify and track Kissinger's particular contribution to Nixon policy is a tricky business. It is made the trickier by Kissinger's way of implying, sometimes by nothing more than a grimace or a tonal nuance, that the record contained in his voluminous and meticulous files may some day show views and positions quite different from those now attributed to him. The safe course for the contemporary chronicler is to assume that United States policy would be little different from what it is if Kissinger were in total charge of it. But, this qualification allowed for, the Kissinger touch and some of the shifts over the past two years in Kissinger's positions can be discerned.

His major contribution to Vietnam and Indochina policy has been the provision and bid for a negotiated settlement. I am convinced that Kissinger calculated in 1969, and led the President to calculate, that Hanoi would choose a negotiated settlement in preference to a prolonged war. The alternative course of "Vietnamization," entailing a gradual and limited shift of combat responsibility to the South Vietnamese, was not expected then to become the only attainable alternative to a rate and kind of withdrawal and to a degree of political concession that Nixon and Kissinger regarded in 1969 and still regard as shameful surrender. Kissinger is said to believe now that Vietnamization has a better chance of success than he thought it had in 1969. But his controlling calculation in that year turned out to be a colossal miscalculation. From the failure to achieve negotiation have flowed the consequences of widened war in Indochina and revived opposition to the war that confront the Administration.

Kissinger's associates do not know to this day whether, in his private discussions with the President, he wholly supported the widening of the war into Cambodia in 1970. What is known is that he was visibly and unusually uncomfortable when he explained and justified that "incursion." The response to subsequent inquiries suggested that he was unhappy not so much with the action itself as with the belligerent rhetoric in Nixon's announcement of the action. Kissinger encouraged the impression that it was intended to have effects beyond Indochina, among other things putting the Soviet government on notice that Nixon is capable of doing the unexpected and therefore should not be baited with avoidable challenges. But he preferred at the time to let the action speak for itself.

An interesting question is whether Kissinger is or will be for validating the Soviet presence in the Middle East by placing American with Soviet forces in an international peace-keeping force. The adopted view would appear to be that the United States is ready to do it, in the unlikely event that Israel is willing. The inquirer gathers, however, that this is State Department and Rogers policy, but not as yet Nixon policy and certainly not Kissinger policy. Although Kissinger's NSC staff has overseen a continuing study of possible American positions in the Middle East, the peace-keeping question has not yet come to the President for decision and Kissinger has not been called upon to declare himself. Henry Kissinger is protecting his options and guarding his

flanks until he comes to the moment of decision, alone with the
President.

April 3, 1971

———

At the end of 1971 the President had yet to indicate a willingness
to commit US forces to a joint peace-keeping role in the Middle East.

XII

Nitty-Gritty
Time

I he trumpet calls for Mr. Nixon's new American revolution are
muted. In the three months since he outlined a substantial program of domestic legislation and proclaimed his purpose to change
the ways and pattern of government with a massive shift of federal power to states and localities, the President has done and
said much less to promote his program and to further the change
than his assistants led the press and the country to expect in
January. It was said then that by now he would have stumped
the land, preaching his revolution and plugging his domestic reforms in person, and that teams of cabinet and sub-cabinet officials
would have taken the message where he didn't have time to go.
Mr. Nixon made only one such trip, to Des Moines. There was
a noticeable lack of regret at the White House when a second foray
to upstate New York was snowed out. A plan to make his visit to
the California White House in late March and early April the
occasion for promotional appearances in the West and along the
Pacific Coast was abandoned at the last moment, again without

discernible sorrow. The war that won't go away, and his sudden
intervention in the Calley case, occupied the President and gave
him an excuse to keep mostly to himself in California. But the
inquirer at the White House senses something deeper than immediate concerns—a change of mood and a steady attrition of ex-
pectations and confidence.

I suspect that a factor in the attrition is a discovery that Mr.
Nixon's assistants have made about him. The discovery is that
Richard Nixon, disclosing himself and explaining himself in an
unprecedented burst of group and individual interviews, and at-
tributing to himself what he has called a Quaker quality of "peace
at the center," is no more understandable and believable and
attractive than the hitherto guarded and, in matters concerning
himself, reticent Nixon was. One must suppose that the discovery
has neither surprised nor disappointed Mr. Nixon, who remarked
during a recent exercise in personal disclosure that he was born
with his image and can't do anything about it. But it has shaken
White House assistants who have been telling reporters for two
years that they would have an improved opinion of the President
if they could see him as he is at work in his Oval Office, likeable
and calm and purposeful and utterly convincing. The charitable
but not, to his apologists, very reassuring conclusion must be that
the private Nixon simply cannot project himself as they see and
know him.

A less esoteric and possibly sounder explanation is to be found
in the dawning recognition at the White House of the realities that
confront the President in Congress. The brief and heady time of
new proposals is past. Now Mr. Nixon and his assistants are im-
mersed in the nitty-gritty of bargaining and compromise that is
necessary in order to get a fair hearing for his proposals in congressional committees and to enhance the generally poor prospects
for favorable floor action in the House and Senate.

The Nixon program of national health insurance is a case in
point. Its core provision is a federal requirement that all employers, large and small, who can by the farthest stretch of the
term be held to affect interstate commerce must provide medical
and hospital insurance for their employes. The employers would
have to pay 60 percent of the cost at first, 75 percent eventually.
Employes would pay the rest. Months of hard and expert study
went into the proposal. With federal payment of the costs for

'YOU'D HAVE HATED THE STEAKS, SO I THREW THEM OUT — HOW ABOUT A GOOD OLD PEANUT BUTTER AND JELLY?'

the poor, the unemployed and the handicapped, it is a bold and advanced proposal, short in both benefits and costs of the totally federalized health program advocated by Senator Kennedy but far ahead of anything in the field that Mr. Nixon's detractors could have expected from him. At this writing, two months after it was submitted to Congress, the President and his staff lobbyists have been unable to persuade a single Republican representative or senator to sponsor and introduce the legislation. John Byrnes of Wisconsin and his junior colleagues on the House Ways and Means Committee, where the fate of the program will be decided, have refused to touch it in its present form because of an outcry from business constituents to the effect the costs will ruin them, force them to fire marginal employes, and have all the dire consequences that the federal minimum wage was once said to threaten. The White House and HEW officials who devised the program are telling the reluctant Republicans that their objections can be met later, by compromises in committee and on the floor, if only they will introduce the legislation as written and give it a chance in competition with the Kennedy and other rival programs. Even if it is introduced, there is little or no hope at the White House that it will emerge from Ways and Means and be enacted as the President offered it. Wilbur Mills is known to be cooking up his own health insurance bill, focused mainly upon federal payment of hospital costs, and that alone could be enough to doom the Nixon plan.

Mr. Mills is responsible in several other respects for a good deal of the White House malaise. Long content with his strategic place at the head of Ways and Means, Chairman Mills is feeling his oats and saying with demure pleasure that he couldn't refuse a convention draft in the exceedingly remote event that the Democrats call upon him to run for the presidency next year. He and the President's assistants are engaged in a game that would be funny if it didn't involve serious public business. The assistants continue to speak of "the chairman" with abject reverence and he keeps assuring them that they and the President are perfectly welcome to claim his bills, when they come out of his committee, as the Administration's own original bills. That is what is happening to Nixon welfare reform, which is undergoing drastic revision in the direction of more stringent work and eligibility requirements and, thanks to Mills, will retain the Nixon label when it is reported from the committee for a House vote. Cynical students of the Mills technique suspect that he is preparing to take credit for permitting the passage of a Nixon program and let Mr. Nixon have credit for the costs, which are thought likely to exceed both the Administration's and the committee's estimates.

The two forms of Nixon revenue and power sharing, "general" and "special," also suffer from the Mills effect. General sharing, with $5 billion initially and $10 billion eventually diverted each year from the federal treasury to state and local governments, must clear the chairman's committee, and his opposition probably means that it never will. Special sharing, lumping previously restricted federal grants for specified purposes into six categories with increased but not total state and local control of the money's use, stands some chance of fragmentary enactment. But there is a note of creeping despair in the White House predictions for it. The most said for it now is that three or perhaps four of the six categories may be approved in some form or other, not necessarily the present Nixon form, over the next two years but maybe not in 1971. The proposed sharing of funds for elementary and secondary education, the last of the six special programs to be submitted, was understood at the White House to be comatose if not actually dead at birth. Shared funds for state and local law enforcement, manpower training, urban and rural development, with some dispersal of control in each instance, are believed to have the best chances, partly because there is a lot of room for compromise in the original proposals and also because, even in the submitted forms, they wouldn't alter present practices and present federal-state relationships nearly as much as the President claims.

The disparity between claim and actuality in this part of the Nixon program is the major source of its troubles and poor prospects in Congress. Too many legislators in both parties understand too well that there is a basically false quality in Nixon revenue (and power) sharing. General sharing, with its recognition of a proven need to assist state and local governments with federal revenue, is a valid and defensible concept. The trouble with it in its Nixon guise, and the reason it has failed to elicit the support it deserves, is that the President and his advisers concluded last year that their budgetary situation did not allow them to come up with enough shared money to make it adequately helpful. In order to put a bigger and theoretically appealing dollar tag on revenue sharing, they thereupon made some changes in the special-purpose grants that already were going to states and localities and called the result "special revenue sharing." The changes were aimed, as the President said, at diminishing federal control and increasing state and local control of the expenditure. That, too, is a defensible concept, although it is subject to legitimate doubts. The merit in it, arguable at best, was not enough to dispel the stink of contrivance and deception that overhangs special revenue sharing. It's tricky, and being tricky is what Mr. Nixon has never been really good at.

April 24, 1971

XIII

Signals to Mao

On February 1, 1969, his twelfth day in office, Mr. Nixon sent a note to Henry Kissinger. The President said that his assistant for national security affairs should explore every means of developing friendly relations with Communist China and should tell East European Communists with whom Kissinger was in touch that this was a very serious purpose of the new administration. Nothing was said about passing the word to Peking, but that of course was the point.

So began what the President, in the 1971 edition of his annual foreign policy review, called "the movement toward normal relations between the United States and the People's Republic of China." It has been a slow movement, too slow for those critics who hold that the US and not the Peking government is principally responsible for the hostility that has prevailed since the Communists took over mainland China in 1949. But there is a rationale for the pace of Mr. Nixon's effort to encourage some movement and lately to hasten it a bit. Because the rationale will continue to govern the Administration's actions and responses to Peking's actions, no matter what the critics in Congress and elsewhere may say, it is set forth here as it was explained to me at the White House and State Department.

The guiding rule is that the American government should do nothing and propose nothing that could invite an explicit rebuff from Peking. The rule arose from a review of China policy that the President ordered four days after he sent the note to Kissinger and that he discussed with the National Security Council on the following May 15. It was a prescription for minimal disturbance of domestic opinion and for minimal political risk, calling as it did for cautious and minor steps toward accommodation that were no more likely to arouse either opposition or public enthusiasm at home than they were to draw an immediate response from Peking. But something more than that must be said for the rule of caution. It was rooted in a judgment that the Peking government would move on its own initiative to improve relations with the US, or respond to American moves toward that end, only when and if such a move or response was considered in Peking to be absolutely necessary and in the vital interest of the People's Republic. In the view thus adopted, the most that the US should try to accomplish was to convince the Peking Communists that, when and if they deemed a favorable move or response to be in their essential interest, the Nixon administration would welcome any sign that they did and would respond within the limits of what it considered to be American necessities and interest.

There followed, beginning in June of 1969, the gradual relaxations of US curbs upon trade with China and travel to China that preceded Peking's invitation to the American table tennis players and Chou En-lai's remark that "a new page" in Chinese-American relations had been turned. This series of Nixon actions had a rather odd history. A long list of actions that the Administration might take without risking the feared rebuff was completed by an interagency study group on July 17, 1969. It included, at least in outline, all of the gestures that have been made since then, including the ones announced by the President on April 14. The most substantial of these, a partial lifting of the embargo on exports to and imports from China, was based upon a list of nonstrategic export items that was compiled for the President last November. A decision as to the items to be allowed and not allowed for export without special license could have been made and the complex regulations implementing the choices could have been drafted at any time since then. But the choices had not been made and the regulations had not been drafted when Mr. Nixon announced the concessions in principle. Similarly, the regulations that will determine how many dollars can be remitted to China for what purposes, in accordance with another of the latest concessions, had not been thought out and prepared. Until the regulations are completed by the bureaucracies at State, Commerce, and Treasury, and approved by the President, nobody can know how much the concessions really amount to.

What they amount to is not, in the White House and State Department view, terribly important. Like the earlier gesures, they are understood to be token actions—signals that the Nixon administration is ready to get down to serious business whenever the Peking government is ready. The important thing, in the Nixon view, is that with its tennis invitation and the admission of a few American correspondents to mainland China the Peking government has signaled back its conclusion, for its own reasons and in its own interest, that a "movement toward normal relations" is in order. By definition, normal relations must in the end require the admission of the People's Republic to the United Nations and diplomatic recognition of the Peking government by the United States. By the generally accepted definition, normal relations in this sense cannot be accomplished until and unless the US is prepared to dump Chiang Kai-shek's "Republic of China" and hand its island home, Taiwan, over to the Chinese Communists. Mr. Nixon is still saying that he will never do that. Peking is still saying that he must. So Mr. Nixon appears to be hooked.

But is he? The hope at the White House, verging upon confident belief, is that he isn't hooked. Or, that, if he is for the moment, the same play of forces and national interest that has led to the current turn toward accommodation will get him off the China hook. Put in simpler fashion than it is put at the White House and State Department, the Nixon hope is that the Peking government will be induced and the Taiwan government will be compelled to resolve their seemingly irreconcilable differences and arrive on their own at the "China solution" of China's problem that many critics of the Administration have advocated.

The basic judgment that Peking would move toward accommo-

dation with the United States only when the Chinese Communists consider accommodation to be essential for them enters importantly into the Nixon calculation. If, the official reasoning runs, the Peking government considers accommodation essential enough to seek or welcome it at all, it must be prepared to pay some price for it. A corollary conclusion is that the worst mistake the US government could make at this point would be to offer the accommodation free of charge. This is why the Administration opposes and predictably will continue to oppose such Senate resolutions as George McGovern's, calling upon the Administration to acknowledge forthwith that the People's Republic is "the sole legitimate government of China" and support its admission to the UN. Why not, the Nixon argument goes, wait at least long enough to find out whether Peking, in return for a developing accommodation with the US, may be willing to set aside the Taiwan issue for a while or perhaps (as Sinologist Doak Barnett has suggested) accept a government restricted to Taiwan as an autonomous affiliate of the People's Republic?

The Administration is closer to a drastic alteration of its relationship with and support of the Taiwan government than is commonly realized. At a press conference on January 29, Secretary of State Rogers was asked whether it is "a fair inference" that the Administration no longer considers the Taiwan government to be the legitimate government of all China. Rogers replied that he would not question the inference. In the President's February foreign policy review, the People's Republic is synonymous with "China." Chiang Kai-shek's Republic of China is synonymous only with Taiwan. In the section of the review dealing with China relations, the President said that "while I cannot foretell the ultimate resolution of the differences between Taipei (Taiwan's capital) and Peking, we believe these differences must be resolved by peaceful means." It was Mr. Nixon's coded way of agreeing with Senator McGovern that "the future status of Taiwan" must eventually be left "to a peaceful resolution by the people on both sides of the Taiwan Straits."

At the President's order, Henry Kissinger in late 1970 conducted intensive interagency studies of the issues and problems connected with the diplomatic recognition of the Peking government and with its surely approaching admission to the UN. The studies have been completed. What they recommend and what

Mr. Nixon will decide after reviewing the findings is unknown. But the fact that they were ordered is sign enough of the President's recognition that Asia is changing and that US policy must change with it.

Vice President Agnew provided another sign of impending change. He griped to a supposedly off-record assemblage of reporters that he was unhappy with and had opposed the trend away from unqualified American support of Taiwan. For the first time since he and Mr. Nixon took office, the White House staff made it known that the President was unhappy with his Vice President's performance.

May 1, 1971

XIV

Panetta's
White House

The White House that Leon Panetta got to know in the 13 months before Mr. Nixon had him fired from his job as the chief civil rights enforcer at the Department of Health, Education, and Welfare turns out in his account of his experience with it (*Bring Us Together*—Lippincott, $5.95) to have been pretty much the kind of place that I and a good many other reporters who observed it from the outside thought it was. Pragmatists, men whose only true dedication was to the political welfare and success of Richard Nixon, dominated the White House staff and were valued elsewhere in government. Zealots, the White House term for officials who were foolish enough to show that some higher conviction moved them, were distrusted and detested. The handling of such matters as public school desegregation, Panetta's main interest, led him to conclude that the explanation for the conduct he observed "might not have been so much abandonment of principles as a lack of principle where domestic issues were concerned." We of the press could deduce that this was true. Leon Panetta and his co-author and former assistant at HEW, Peter Gall, came to know that it was true in their time. Most of the White House characters who taught them that it was true are still there, doing what they did in 1969 and early 1970. It's the same Nixon White House, except that presidential 1972 is nearer than it was and that political considerations are, if anything, more compelling than they were in the first months.

Panetta, a lawyer from California, and Gall, a journalist from Michigan, are Republicans. Their story is principally Panetta's, with Gall identified as co-author and treated in the third person. They were staff assistants to Republican Senator Thomas H. Kuchel of California when he was defeated for renomination in 1968. Panetta, than 30, and Gall, then 33, had their doubts about both Nixon and Robert H. Finch, the California lieutenant governor who was to be HEW Secretary and their boss. They suspected that Finch, after his long association with Nixon, "might well share some of his ability to walk too fine a line between principle and politics." Nixon's campaign promises, implied and stated, to conciliate the South by slowing down civil rights enforcement bothered them. But they had been impressed by Nixon's post-election pledge to "bring us together again." They didn't believe that any President, even Nixon, could turn back the clock and refuse to enforce the law. "You somehow wanted the Administration to work, even if you weren't crazy about the chief." So they joined up, Panetta first as a special assistant to Secretary Finch and then as director of HEW's Office for Civil Rights, and Gall as his press spokesman at OCR.

They were on the fringe of White House operations. But the Panetta office was at the center of White House concerns. It shared with the Justice Department the duty of enforcing both the Supreme Court's 1954 finding that deliberate segregation by race in publicly supported schools violates the Constitution and the statutory requirement that federal funds must be withheld from deliberately segregated schools and school districts. Panetta proposed to enforce the law, period. Nixon and Attorney General John N. Mitchell proposed to enforce it, too, but always in a manner that would cause the least possible disturbance to white Southern voters.

Conflict was inevitable, Bob Finch was caught between the White House and his enforcers, and the Panetta account presents a saddening record of the erosion of confidence and courage that preceded Finch's transfer in June of 1970 from HEW to the White House staff. Panetta writes of Finch as he was the day he let his OCR director be fired at Nixon's order: "In fact, the Secretary had stood by me many times. He was sensitive to the [desegregation] issue. But I had come to a reluctant conclusion some months before that he would never fully use the key position he held, the potential power he had within the Administration to speak up for the nonpolitical solution to civil rights enforcement."

One of Panetta's early introductions to the pressures that all but destroyed Finch was at a meeting of Southern Republican chairmen in Washington. Peter Flanigan, a Nixon assistant whose responsibilities were not known to include civil rights, was telling the politicians when Panetta entered: "It takes time to clean out a government, and we're working at it. . . . It'll take time to clean out the lower-level bureaucrats." Panetta, the recently recruited lower-level bureaucrat, tried to convince his audience that he was as anxious as anyone else in the Administration to enforce the law through "voluntary compliance" and friendly communication where and when that was possible. Former Congressman Howard (Bo) Calloway of Georgia retorted, "The law, the law—listen here. Nixon promised the South he would change the law, change the Supreme Court, and change this whole integration business. The time has come for Nixon to bite the bullet, with real changes and none of this communicating bullshit." Harry Dent of South Carolina, who had shifted from Senator Strom Thurmond's service to Nixon's, told the same group at a later meeting and in Panetta's hearing that "we're marching right ahead and everything looks good. Just give us a little time, and we'll have everything worked out."

John D. Ehrlichman, Nixon's assistant for domestic affairs and the chief staff overseer of school affairs, invited Panetta to lunch in the White House mess. Bryce Harlow, the staff counselor in charge of congressional liaison, joined them. Ehrlichman, a lawyer, pretended to know less than he did about civil rights legalities and asked why the minority of Southern school districts still in total noncompliance couldn't have "a little more time." Panetta's reply that they'd had all the time since 1954 and that the Supreme Court was getting impatient did not appear to impress Ehrlichman. He extracted a promise that the White House staff would be notified before any districts were denied federal funds. Harlow, talking as if he were oblivious of the historic differences between

Northern and Southern segregation, argued that "what we should do is bring all of this integration business to a stop in the South until the North catches up." Panetta remembers that he thought to himself, "My God, he really means it—he really means it." Finch, alarmed by what he heard of the lunch from Nixon assistants, told his departmental staff that "they think Panetta is really a superzealot . . . nothing but a bloodthirsty integrationist."

A critical issue in May 1969 involved 21 of Senator Thurmond's South Carolina districts and a court order that they submit acceptable compliance plans to HEW. The White House hoped to demonstrate the validity of its "voluntary" approach by persuading the districts to adopt plans drawn up by HEW instead of inviting final court action or the administrative termination of their federal money. Only two districts had capitulated. Finch told Panetta that "the President himself was getting antsy about those South Carolina districts." Nixon had suggested that he and Finch go to South Carolina and see what they could do. Panetta and the Secretary's executive assistant, Patrick Gray, convinced Finch that he and Nixon would compound the confusion and further weaken the desegregation effort if they intervened. John Mitchell settled the matter by requiring HEW and persuading the court to allow the holdouts an extra year, until the fall of 1970 instead of 1969, to come into token compliance.

So things went until the end for Panetta. He gave more than a little; Finch gave a lot. Nothing they did could satisfy Nixon's people so long as Panetta and his enforcers were upsetting the white South and keeping the President in a condition of intermittent fury. Finch and HEW Under Secretary John Veneman stood off a flat White House demand for Panetta's resignation in September. On February 17, 1970, a Washington newspaper reported that "congressional sources" had word directly from the White House that Panetta was going to be fired. While Finch, confronted by Panetta, was trying by telephone to get confirmation or a denial from the White House, Press Secretary Ronald Ziegler announced that "Mr. Panetta has submitted his resignation to Secretary Finch." Panetta, weeping at one point, submitted his resignation five hours afterward. With a handshake and in silence, Finch accepted it.

May 8, 1971

XV

Reagan's Welfare Deal

After a conference at San Clemente on April 2 with his rival for the presidency in 1968, Governor Ronald Reagan of California, Mr. Nixon walked out of the western White House with Reagan and HEW Secretary Elliot Richardson and said that he and they had "just completed one of the most constructive meetings on the problem of welfare reform that I have attended." At their "summit conference on welfare reform," the President said, he and Reagan had found "many areas of agreement" and had established to their mutual satisfaction that "major details" of the governor's proposals to tighten restrictions and cut the costs of welfare in California "can be implemented without being in violation or contrary to the federal regulations or federal law." Mr. Nixon said twice that he and his guest were working together "toward a common goal" and then left the governor and the secretary to answer the questions of reporters.

The occasion reeked of a deal. Reagan and Richardson showed by their manifest embarrassment that they knew the reporters knew that it did, and events since then have made the nature of the deal very plain. The same events indicate that the President is getting the short end of his bargain with the governor. In return for a qualified and deceptive profession of support for Nixon's national welfare program, Reagan has what amounts to the President's guarantee, in advance of the review on the merits that is supposed to precede federal approval of the kind of changes intended in California, that the most important of the changes will be approved because the President wants them approved. The required review is proceeding at HEW, with a show of independence granted to Secretary Richardson by the President and by Richardson to the concerned subordinates. Reagan's welfare officials in Sacramento are aflutter with alarm that some of his proposals may not be approved in the submitted forms, and the Democrats who control the legislature are using this possibility as an excuse to oppose necessary changes in state laws.

But there is an aura of farce over the whole performance. It is being conducted in Washington in what has come to be the classic Nixon fashion, and it is not a pretty thing to watch. Elliot Richardson, who personifies all there is of personal and official integrity in the Nixon administration, let himself be committed ahead of the factual review to the proposition that there was "really no problem" with 38 of the 66 Reagan proposals and that most of the ones that do present some difficulty entail "no significant problem" because "they are consistent with the Administration's own welfare proposals." The President leaves the details of following the HEW review to his assistant for domestic affairs, John Ehrlichman, who in turn leaves them to two of his principal deputies, Edward L. Morgan and Edwin L. Harper. Morgan and Harper gave a Reagan welfare team a hearing at the White House in March. Ehrlichman, Morgan and Harper require only that the reviewing officials at HEW "keep them informed," which is a Nixon euphemism for the understood rule that the department officials are not to make a move before they check with the White House staff. There have been two meetings in Sacramento and two in Washington between HEW officials and their state counterparts. Reagan spelled out his proposals on March 3 in a lengthy message to the legislature, with explicit references to the key changes that neither he nor the legislature can put into effect until and unless HEW waives the federal laws and regulations that ordinarily prohibit the intended practices.

Yet Secretary Richardson and his subordinates pretend that they can't really know what the major Reagan proposals are or decide what to do about them until formal requests for the necessary waivers are submitted. There is something to that claim. But the protective emphasis and reliance placed upon it suggest that the secretary and his people are troubled by their part in the business and wish it could be left to the President and his assistants.

It would be a mistake, however, to assume that the President is merely trying with his end of the deal to keep Reagan off his back in 1972 and that Reagan is merely trying to curry favor with the middle Americans in California and elsewhere who respond favorably to his (and Nixon's) continual intimations that most people who go on welfare are willful bums. The President and the governor do have "a common goal"; it is a goal that has to be taken seriously, and Nixon and Reagan are quite correct when they say that their national and state proposals for "welfare reform" fit nicely in many respects. The goal is to halt the rise in welfare rolls and to bring the costs of welfare under control. Governor Nelson Rockefeller of New York, who is usually thought to be the Republican opposite of Ronald Reagan, shares the goal and has persuaded his legislature to enact several changes aimed at attaining it. In order to implement the changes, he is asking HEW for federal waivers similar to some of the ones that Reagan needs. Rockefeller is said to have been somewhat abashed when the President recently bracketed him with Reagan and thanked them "for biting a bullet the entire country is going to have to bite." There are large differences between the Reagan approach and the more humane Rockefeller approach. But the two governors have a tacit understanding that they are working toward the same end, Rockefeller pressing for more federal money to pay the costs while Reagan presses for changes to reduce the costs, and neither could have been greatly surprised when Mr. Nixon commended both of them "for their efforts in this area."

One of Reagan's changes would cast out a requirement that state and local governments, in determining eligibility for welfare, exclude $30 for work expenses and one third of an applicant's earned income from the base that governs the decision whether he or she is entitled to help. Another Reagan proposal would eliminate most of the additional allowances for the expenses of working that, in proclaimed Nixon doctrine, constitute a valued incentive to get people "off the welfare rolls and onto payrolls." Others— these are only representative samples—would sharply reduce the cash and property reserves that welfare recipients may keep against emergency need or for personal use; impose a flat and greatly reduced ceiling upon the amount that a welfare recipient may earn without total disqualification; and require employable adults to labor at made-work "public assistance jobs" for the equivalent of their welfare payment if they are found unfit for available private or government jobs at regular wages. A related proposal, approved in principle by HEW, would require welfare and other beneficiaries of federally supported state medical aid to pay token charges in order to discourage the demand for publicly provided medical services.

Underlying practically all of the Reagan proposals, and pervading the language in which he presents them, is the attitude that people on welfare simply should not enjoy the amenities that non-welfare people enjoy. Reagan promises higher rather than reduced benefits for "the truly needy" and statistically supports the claim that his program would have that effect. His definition of "the truly needy" is extremely harsh and narrow. It goes as far as he evidently thinks the federal government will allow toward excluding those who can or do work for pay, at wages near or below the sparse federal and state standards of need. The prior assurances that Reagan has wrung from the Administration do not absolutely guarantee that all of his changes will be approved to the extent and in exactly the way he asks. But HEW officials acknowledge in a tone of distinct discomfort that the secretary is authorized to approve most of them, including the ones that on their face stretch the law to its outer limits.

There is a certain satisfaction to be had from watching Richard Nixon being taken by Ronald Reagan and it is just possible that the President may derive a needed lesson from the experience. He is committed to approving the "major details" of the Reagan program. Reagan is committed to nothing. For all of his talk about cooperating with Mr. Nixon in getting "welfare reform at the national level," Reagan remains adamant in his opposition to a guaranteed federal floor under the incomes of dependent families and to the inclusion as a matter of national policy of underpaid "working poor" among those who are eligible for federal and state welfare support. Without these elements, the Nixon program would be as harsh and inhuman as the Reagan "reform" is in its worst aspects.

May 15, 1971

———

HEW approved the chief departures from federal standards wanted by Reagan and Rockefeller. They fared better with their legislatures than the President did with Congress, which let a third year pass without meaningful action on welfare reform.

XVI

Civil Rights Report

The US Commission on Civil Rights has just experienced and demonstrated the difficulty of being kind to Richard Nixon. "I don't go for scapegoats, I don't think it's fair to put it all on one man," the commission's chairman, the Reverend Theodore M. Hesburgh, said at a press conference in Washington. His point was that the total society and the whole bureaucracy shared with the President the responsibility for the facts and attitudes that caused the commission to conclude, in the first of a series of periodic progress reports, that "the federal government is not yet in a position to claim that it is enforcing the letter, let alone the spirit, of civil rights laws." Some of the reporters at the press conference refused to buy that line or to be impressed by Father Hesburgh's plea that "it's easy to get headlines if you say the President is a bum" instead of holding to the duller view that "it's a matter of the whole system." They tried again and again to make him and the five commissioners who were sitting with him say, as they had said in a previous critique of the federal effort, that accomplishment in civil rights "depends on the quality of leadership exercised by the President" and that the missing factor was "courageous moral leadership." The chairman, discernibly uncomfortable in his role of the President's protector, acknowledged that the necessary leadership was still lacking and had to "come from the top." One of the commission's two black members, Mrs. Frankie Freeman, said that "there has not been aggressive leadership on the part of the President and the federal government." Commissioner Maurice B. Mitchell, a white educator, said that "it's going to take much more pressure than the President is exerting" and pleased the clamorous reporters with his remark that "you are quite right when you exude a sense of cynicism."

The events that followed the commission's earlier critique and preceded its latest report on federal progress induce a mixed sense of cynicism and wonder. The cynicism arises from the evidence in both reports that the Nixon administration is incapable of the "comprehensive and total action" that the commission continues to demand. The wonder is that the record cited by the commission is no worse than it is and that a few Nixon assistants, serving an administration that accords civil rights a higher priority in its rhetoric than in its actions, were able to encourage and in some instances to bring about what the commission called "a number of positive changes" in the seven months under review. The only change credited directly to the President was "a substantial across-the-board increase" in funds budgeted for civil rights personnel and enforcement in fiscal 1972. Two of his assistants, Special Consultant Leonard Garment and George P. Shultz, the director of the Office of Management and Budget, appeared to the commission to be its particular and most effective friends at the White House. Without their "active intervention" and assertion of "personal interest," the commission said, some of the positive changes that it noted would not have occurred. One of the changes, due in part to quiet pressure from Garment, was the beginning of recognition by the Securities and Exchange Commission, the Interstate Commerce Commission, the Civil Aeronautics Board and the Federal Home Loan Bank Board that they have or conceivably may have some responsibility for the racial policies and practices of the industries and enterprises they regulate. Garment and Shultz are the President's men, their only power is his delegated power, and in this sense their intervention was his intervention. On some occasions, it is said at the White House, they acted for positive change only after consulting Mr. Nixon and with his specific assent. Beyond that generalization, assistants who were invited to specify and document examples of the President's personal and positive actions in behalf of civil rights would not go. In the only instances I was able to pin down, Mr. Nixon's influence was negative.

These instances had to do with federal action to encourage or require suburban integration and with the Civil Rights Commission's insistence that the traditional merit system must be substantially modified if black and other minority employes are to get a fair shake in federal hiring and promotion. Mr. Nixon forbade any departure whatever, in White House and departmental responses to the Civil Rights Commission, from his declared position against "forced integration" of any kind and against federal action to require the "economic integration" of all-white suburbs. In the selection of sites for federal offices and other installations, and in the conditions attached to federally subsidized housing, the General Services Administration and the Department of Housing and Urban Development were forbidden to indicate to the Civil Rights Commission that they will put any more than the minimal emphasis they put now upon fair and open residential policies. Mr. Nixon went along with a recommendation that the Civil Service Commission *allow* federal agencies, including his own Office of Management and Budget, to set numerical goals for minority hiring and promotion and to fix timetables for meeting the goals. At George Shultz's strong urging, and with the President's approval, OMB has increased the number of black employes in professional grades from 11 to 33, in the last six months. But the President balked at the Civil Rights Commission's view that the Civil Service Commission should *require* what amounts to minority hiring and promotion quotas, though nobody calls them that. A tepid and permissive directive was still in preparation at the Civil Service Commission long after the Civil Rights Commission had been told that it had already gone out to all federal agencies.

Two of the positive changes occurred within Mr. Nixon's own shop. His Cabinet Committee on Education, set up last year to further "voluntary" school desegregation in the South, was enlarged and transformed into a permanent Committee on Civil Rights, attached to the President's Domestic Council. All that was missing, as the commission noted, was a clearly defined mission for the new committee. Mumblings at the White House indicate that it will function on an *ad hoc* basis, handling any particular jobs the President may assign to it. When Mr. Nixon and assorted counselors finally decide what to do in the aftermath of the recent Supreme Court decisions, calling for expanded busing and other measures to complete school desegregation in the urban South, the committee may be used as its predecessor was to diminish white resistance and the consequent political harm. A logical task for the committee would be to formulate a clear and forceful civil rights policy. As Leonard Garment told the Civil Rights Commission, however, the need is not recognized at the White House. Just read Mr. Nixon's speeches and statements on civil rights, Garment said, and the policy will be perfectly plain. That is correct. The essence is that the law does not allow what the law does not require, a formulation that permits a narrow range of civil rights action and amounts to an abdication of presidential responsibility.

The other White House action that the commission applauded within limits was the acceptance by Shultz and OMB of "a leadership role in civil rights enforcement." This means, in theory and perhaps in fact, that the enormous powers of the budgetary process will be brought to bear upon departmental and agency practices and policies affecting civil rights. In memoranda dating back to last October, Shultz has instructed his senior assistants and the 150 OMB examiners who review agency budget requests to demand positive evidence that the requirements of law and of presidential policy are being met in civil rights matters, and that each agency has both the will and the manpower necessary to meet them. That's fine, the Civil Rights Commission says in response, but it can't amount to much until and unless Shultz establishes a Civil Rights Division in OMB and entrusts the oversight function to dedicated civil rights specialists instead of to OMB career officials. This the President and Shultz refuse to do. They are not about to vest that kind of power in people who bring to civil rights enforcement the passion the Civil Rights Commission tries to evoke.

May 22, 1971

———

In another report in November 1971, the Civil Rights Commission found the administration still failing to provide adequate and vigorous leadership. The Cabinet Committee on Civil Rights remained comatose and invisible throughout 1971. The courts compelled more action to open up segregated suburbs than the President wanted to take.

XVII

Busing
and Politics

Mr. Nixon summoned Attorney General Mitchell and HEW Secretary Richardson to the White House for a private talk on April 21. The subject was the unanimous Supreme Court finding, announced the day before in two cases from North Carolina and Alabama, that the Constitution requires much more stringent and extensive measures to eliminate the remnants of racial segregation in the South's public schools than the President has thought either wise or necessary. All that is known of the discussion is that the President asked the Attorney General how he interpreted the decisions and told Mitchell and Richardson that he relied upon them to solve the problems the court had made for the Administration. It may be supposed, however, that Mr. Nixon restated in one way or another the rule that he imposed upon the federal enforcers of school desegregation soon after he took office. According to a White House assistant who is involved in the enforcement process, the Nixon rule is: "Do what you have to do, but don't raise any more hell than you have to when you do it."

Mitchell, Richardson, several White House assistants and subordinate officials at HEW and the Justice Department proceeded in the next four weeks to devise a response to the Supreme Court's decisions that would comply alike with them and with the Nixon rule. The response that emerged was in the form of a letter from HEW to the Austin, Texas school board, with a copy to the federal district court in Austin. The letter invited the court to require the Austin board, as urban school authorities throughout the South must eventually be required, to go a great deal further than the board had proposed to go in breaking up the city's pattern of neighborhood schools, busing black and Mexican-American children from their home neighborhoods to white neighborhoods and schools, and busing white children from their neighborhoods into black and Mexican-American neighborhoods and schools. It is for the federal courts to say whether the HEW suggestions, combined with those already volunteered by the Austin board, satisfy the Supreme Court's criteria. But the HEW response seems to this layman to be a strong scheme for real desegregation. It calls for interneighborhood busing and other desegregation measures of a kind and on a scale that Mr. Nixon led the South, in 1968 and well into 1970, to believe it would never have to suffer so long as he had anything to do with the definition and enforcement of the law. The President had no choice, of course, but to make at least a show of compliance with the Supreme Court's decisions. He allowed his subordinates to do considerably more than that in the Austin letter, knowing as they knew that it was to be the approximate model for the Administration posture in the many other Southern cities and larger towns where previously proposed or approved compliance plans must be similarly revised.

The story of how the Austin response came into being is not a story that the Administration's guiding minds particularly want told. About all that's left of Mr. Nixon's Southern Strategy, after two years of battering at it by the federal courts, is the impression among his white constituents in the South that he and his Attorney General and his HEW Secretary are reluctant enforcers of the laws and decisions requiring a total end to officially imposed racial segregation in the schools. That is why the President tells his enforcers to raise minimum hell in the South and says at every opportunity, in his public version of the Nixon rule, that he proposes to accomplish the required compliance by "cooperation rather than coercion." The facts hardly demonstrate anything that civil rights activists and believers in the basic rightness of desegregated education would call enthusiasm for the cause. But the federal courts' steady expansion of the legal requirement is actually less painful to the President and his senior counselors than they prefer to have journalists and others say it is. The Nixon enforcers, beginning with Attorney General Mitchell, welcome any development that tends to get the President and his Administration off the desegregation hook. They figure that this is what the Supreme Court and lower federal courts do when they, rather than the executive agencies, broaden the legal requirement. "Court decisions," a Justice Department official remarked last week, "can be very handy things."

A syndicated report of a meeting that Mitchell had at HEW with Richardson and other department officials on the same day he and the secretary conferred with Nixon illustrates the point. The report had it that Mitchell barged in upon the Richardson staff and, in a knockdown argument with HEW officials, demanded the slowest and most grudging response to the Supreme Court decisions that could be devised. Nothing of the sort occurred. The meeting was called for another purpose, the court decisions were mentioned only in passing, and Mitchell said nothing to discourage the preparation of an adequate compliance plan. Mitchell later told the responsible columnist that he was "180 degrees wrong," but he and his official spokesmen did nothing else to correct a widely published report. Mr. Nixon's spokesmen at the White House didn't lift a finger to correct a report that a similar confrontation occurred at a meeting of the President's Cabinet Committee on Education. The Court decisions were explained at that meeting, but there was no argument worth mentioning about the proper response. There was nothing to argue about: the inevitable decision to comply had been made, and the only question was how to do it without raising avoidable hell in Austin and elsewhere in the South.

Secretary Richardson and two other HEW officials, General Counsel Wilmot Hastings and Civil Rights Director Stanley Pottinger, submitted HEW's Austin plan to Mitchell at the Justice Department on May 12, three days before it had to be delivered to the Austin court. More than one junior official at HEW and

Justice had predicted that Mitchell would never go for the recommended degree of busing and other desegregation measures. Like
many other officials at the Administration's working levels, they
had precisely the image of the President and the Attorney General
that much of the public has. In this instance, Mitchell proved them
wrong. He heard out a cold-turkey presentation of the details,
agreed with Richardson that there was no practicable alternative,
and rejected a suggestion from one of his own subordinates that
less of the busing burden could be placed upon the white students
in Austin's affluent sections and more of it upon the poorer whites
who live near the black and Mexican-American sections.

Later that day, Hastings and Pottinger submitted the plan at the
White House to Edward L. Morgan, the assistant who is charged
by Nixon with coordinating and overseeing every Administration
move on civil rights. Morgan made a change that was typically in
keeping with the Nixon rule. Why not, he said, deliver the plan to
Austin in the form of a friendly and flattering commentary upon
the local board's previously submitted plan, rather than as HEW's
complete and probably offensive alternative to the local plan? At
the eleventh hour before a response had to be delivered to the
Austin court, somebody at HEW thought of satisfying the court in
two easy stages, first with a brief notice of intent to submit HEW's
views and afterward with the HEW recommendations. Mitchell,
asked what he thought of that idea, said he preferred to do it all
at once. The Supreme Court had spoken on this issue, he said,
and he wasn't going to play around with it.

Now the Administration's elaborate apparatus for conciliation,
with the Cabinet Committee on Civil Rights at the top and seven
biracial state committees in support, is gearing up to minimize the
expectable hell. One of the conciliators is Harry Dent of South
Carolina, the President's staff specialist in southern sensibilities and
votes. Another is the Reverend Richard Scott Brannan, a Dent
protégé in the personal service of Secretary Richardson. Brannan
is a Southern Baptist minister whose last pastorate was at Dent's
church in Columbia. His job at HEW, as a special assistant to the
Secretary, is to receive unhappy Southerners on Richardson's behalf and convince them, if he can, that the Nixon Administration
is doing to them only what the courts and the law compel it to do.
It is not a noble or ennobling technique. But the same general
approach brought about more desegregation in the South in 1970

than anybody had reason to expect from Richard Nixon. If it works again, I for one won't be complaining.

May 29, 1971

———

On the following August 3, Mr. Nixon taught me that it is foolish *ever* to assume his good faith in a matter as politically sensitive as school desegregation and busing (see Chapter XXV).

XVIII

With Cheops in
Texas

Austin

While Mr. Nixon spoke at the dedication of the Lyndon Baines Johnson Library and School of Public Affairs on the University of Texas campus, emitting platitudes that he had tried out a few days earlier on a group of visiting politicians at the White House, LBJ put on a classic Johnsonian performance in his seat to the President's rear and left. A beholder was reminded of Johnson at the Democratic convention in 1964, stealing the show while Hubert Humphrey accepted the nomination for the vice presidency. The performance this time was not so blatant, not at all in the wretched taste of the antics in Atlantic City. This was Johnson's day and he was entitled to claim every moment of it for himself. But one perceived that the big man in the tan suit hadn't changed very much in the 28 months since Richard Nixon followed him in the White House and had every portable relic of the Johnson presence —desk, news tickers, TV sets—ejected overnight from the Oval Office. Johnson in retirement had let himself run to fat: when he escorted President and Mrs. Nixon to the library, and later to the platform on a lawn in front of it, and when he moved in triumph among his 3000 guests on the adjacent grounds, he walked with the slow and cautious waddle of a compulsive eater who has allowed his torso to grow too heavy for his ankles. Seated and enduring his successor's droned clichés, however, he was altogether the remembered and unchanging LBJ, a figure in scale with the monumental marble pile of the library looming behind him and Nixon.

As the President began ("honored to be here, deep in the heart of Texas"), Johnson hunkered on his chair, hands on his thighs, glancing downward and to his right, away from Nixon, a look of sardonic amusement commanding the notice of all who watched the spectacle. His expression invited the unseemly thought that he might have been dreaming up and relishing another of the scatological references to some aspects of Nixon domestic policy that guests at the round of dedication parties gleefully attributed to him. He squirmed; he fidgeted. He reached for a jacket pocket and snatched his hand back to rest upon his thigh. When the President quoted Albert Beveridge, a turn-of-the-century senator and orator from Indiana, to the rather foggy effect that "the partisan of principle is a prince of citizenship," Johnson looked as if he had read the advance text and knew what was coming. He gazed at the low clouds overhead, then at the magnificent stand of trees on a hilltop opposite his library, and again at the clouds. Toward the dreary end he leaned right and left, peering past Nixon and grimacing genially at friends and associates from his great days who were there by the hundreds to evoke their great days with him.

At the very end, when Nixon approached his mercifully final reference to "partisans of principle," Johnson fell into vigorous and visibly admonitory converse with Frank C. Erwin, Jr., a rich Texan who until recently was chairman of the university regents and presided at the ceremonies. Erwin introduced Julie and David Eisenhower and the Johnson daughters, with their husbands and children, and the Johnson face glowed with utter delight when Luci Johnson Nugent held up his grandson, "Little Lyn." It was, one judged, the first moment that Johnson had wholly enjoyed since he finished his own speech, a short and gracious promise that the 31 million documents in his library will in time (it will be a long, long time) disclose the truth "with the bark off" about his career and his presidency.

'STOP LOOKIN' AT ME LIKE THAT — THIS IS THE **TRUTH** I'M READIN' Y'ALL!'

Erwin, Johnson, Nixon and the Texas Democratic Party's gift to the Nixon Administration, Treasury Secretary John Connally, kept their heads bowed in assumable approval when the Reverend George Richard Davis of Washington, DC, a mousey man in black who was seated on the platform beside Vice President Agnew, called down God's benediction "upon this great university, not as yet frozen in the glacier of pseudointellectualism." Agnew was seen to address Davis very warmly indeed when he returned to his seat. His reference was one of several indicators of the campus tensions which have resulted in part from the restrictive policies of the Erwin faction on the board of regents and have caused the flight of some of the university's faculty stars. Black balloons launched by antiwar students scudded overhead while the Reverend Billy Graham, who had flown to Austin on the President's plane, rapped out his steely thanks to God for giving the nation two such leaders as Johnson and Nixon. Several hundred students and other protesters, barred from the dedication area by police, raised a racket during the ceremonies and perpetrated some minor trashing after Nixon left.

The reporters who accompanied Nixon were inclined to minimize the signs of strain and settle for the verdict that it was a memorable and unique day. They were right: even the huge library building and School of Public Affairs beside it turned out upon inspection not to be the vulgar excesses that some news accounts had depicted. No doubt the library, its solid marble walls curving upward from a massive marble base, will continue to be dubbed "Lyndon's Pyramid." But it fits him and Texas and the rolling campus land. This visitor found himself unable to begrudge LBJ the millions of university dollars that went into it and the million or so of federal money that the library will cost annually to administer. The test will be whether Johnson in his remaining lifetime is fair and generous in his grant of access to the documentary treasures and trivia it contains. Law and the National Archives are supposed to govern access to presidential libraries, but the ex-Presidents for whom the libraries are built are in fact the controllers while they live and Johnson will have to be more generous than Harry Truman has been in Missouri if scholars are to be content with the LBJ Library. Johnson probably will be generous. It was announced at the ceremony that he and Lady Bird contributed some $2 million of their money to the library's cost. He likes to

have people, scholars presumably included, in thrall and debt to
him.

The reporters with Nixon, watching him depart after his duty
was done for a weekend in Key Biscayne and then for a day's
politicking in Alabama, speculated among themselves that he must
be wondering how to top Lyndon's Pyramid with *his* memorial
library. His spokesmen joked, rather uneasily, that he has another
five years to ponder that problem. I'd guess that it won't be much
of a problem. Nixon is the kind of man and President whose way of
topping LBJ will be to call into being an ostentatiously modest
library structure pointing up in the time to come the differences
between him and LBJ. The differences were apparent in Austin.
If Nixon, standing in sober garb at the podium and speaking with
deliberate dullness, sensed the act that the big man behind him
was putting on, he probably didn't object. He could have welcomed
it as a reminder to the audience and to the country that his way
of quiet order has its uses after a time of extravagant and, in part,
disastrous presidential splendor.

June 5, 1971

XIX

More
Desegregation

The President continued last week to let his underlings in the Departments of Justice and Health, Education and Welfare behave as if there were no Southern Strategy and as if he enjoyed enforcing the law in the way the Supreme Court says he must. There still is a Southern Strategy, reduced though it largely is to assuring white Southerners that this-hurts-me-more-than-it-hurts-you, and it cannot be believed that Mr. Nixon relishes the degree of public school desegregation that he is now compelled to ask the lower federal courts to compel him to require in school districts where the remnants of legally imposed racial segregation persist. But, however cynically the process of enforcement may be viewed and explained, it is gathering momentum, and liberal critics of the Administration may as well face the fact that their image of the President in this regard is outdated.

The Administration's first response on May 14 to the Supreme Court's expanded mandate of April 20 left open the possibility that the tough requirements for more desegregation and more busing in the Austin, Texas, school district might be bargained away in private discussions between HEW and Justice officials and the Austin authorities. That possibility vanished when Jack Davidson, Austin's superintendent of schools, visited Washington with the president of his school board, Will Davis, and the board's attorney, J. M. Patterson, Jr. Neither HEW Secretary Elliot Richardson nor Attorney General John Mitchell nor Edward L. Morgan, the White House assistant who monitors school enforcement for the President, deigned to meet them. The senior HEW officials who did were General Counsel Wilmot Hastings and Civil Rights Director Stanley Pottinger. David Norman, acting civil rights director at Justice, represented Mitchell. The Austin delegation pleaded that the HEW plan submitted to the federal district court in Austin would require the purchase and manning of 240 additional buses and a first-year increase of more than $2 million in public expense, and impair rather than improve the quality of education in a disrupted school system. The complainants had the theoretically persuasive backing of Texas' two senators, Republican John Tower and Democrat Lloyd Bentsen, powerful figures in a state that Mr. Nixon needs in order to win reelection in 1972. The plea and the political support were in vain, as might have been foreseen from the terms in which the senators had expressed their objections. Tower, taking his cue from the White House, put the onus on the federal courts rather than upon the Administration. Bentsen denounced HEW's alleged lack of courtesy and consultation in its earlier dealings with the Austin district, not the HEW plan in itself. Pottinger refused to budge on essential points and the Austin group, despairing of help from Washington, went home prepared to fight out the issue in court.

Next on the enforcement list were Nashville, Tenn., and another Texas district, Corpus Christi. In both, as in Austin, federal district judges had done the Administration the favor of ordering it to submit HEW-Justice alternatives to local board compliance plans. Secretary Richardson and Pottinger checked out their Nashville and Corpus Christi recommendations, as they had checked their Austin plan, with Mitchell at a meeting in his office on May 25. Again, as in the pilot discussions of the Austin plan, Mitchell approved desegregation measures that went far beyond what the local school authorities proposed. In Nashville, under a plan that met HEW requirements before the Supreme Court invalidated them with its April 20 decisions, more than half of the black students attend high schools with 90 percent or higher black enrollments, and nearly half of the black elementary students are in 10 schools attended by only 78 white students. The combined Nashville and Davidson County school district proposed to improve but not eliminate this situation by busing 35,600 elementary and secondary students to schools outside their neighborhoods. HEW asked the federal district court in Nashville to require the busing of 49,000 students in a pattern that would eliminate all instead of some majority-black schools. A softer alternative that would have left one majority-black high school was discarded before it was submitted either to Mitchell or to the Nashville court. In similar fashion, the milder of two alternative plans for Corpus Christi was discarded within HEW. Forty-nine percent of Corpus Christi's public school students are Mexican-Americans and 6 percent are black, making a "minority" total of 55 percent, and 80 percent of all "minority" pupils are in schools attended mostly by students of their own kind. HEW asked the federal court to establish a system-wide racial ratio that corresponds approximately to the community ratio.

Tougher situations, from the Administration's standpoint, remain to be dealt with in Southern urban districts that are under court order but have not as yet been called upon by the controlling district or appellate courts to amend their present attendance patterns. The word from Attorney General Mitchell in regard to these school districts is to let the concerned courts take the initiative. As of June 2, his civil rights division hadn't heard of any such initiatives being taken and was not about to prod the responsible judges into action.

The most difficult situations are in the relatively few urban districts of the South that previously chose to meet HEW's standards, now outmoded, without going to court. One such is in Columbia, the capital city of Senator Strom Thurmond's South Carolina, where less than half of the black students are in majority-white schools and many schools that are nearly or entirely all white and all black survive. HEW, Justice and White House officials know quite well where the others are—to all effects, they are the urban and semi-urban Southern districts that are not under court order.

The officials in question, principally Secretary Richardson and Attorney General Mitchell, nevertheless were having an awful time trying to decide how to put these pesky districts on notice that they have to make some changes. Large amounts of high-level executive time and energy went into arguments over whether to write directly to the superintendents of each affected school district or to put the monkey on state Superintendents of Education by asking them to tell the local officials that HEW and Justice will be after them if they don't volunteer more desegregation than they have tolerated so far. How to use the President's recently enlarged Cabinet Committee on Education and its affiliated biracial state committees to further compliance with the new standards at minimum political cost was also a subject of intense official discussion. The result in early June was little more than a conviction that there ought to be some way to accomplish the necessary changes without irretrievably alienating white Southern voters in disastrous numbers. If there is a way, it is through continued reliance upon the courts to do the dirty work, and this rather than administrative termination of federal school funds will in most if not all instances be the chosen way.

As I have reported, the Administration does not welcome public emphasis upon its readiness to take the court route when the law requires it. A positive effort is necessary in order to extract from the Mitchell Justice Department the details of its record in this respect. No general announcement, other than legally required publication in the widely unread *Federal Register,* accompanied the Attorney General's recent issuance of guidelines that on their face should strengthen his hitherto weak enforcement of the Voting Rights Act. Between February 5 and May 28, the Justice Department initiated or joined other plaintiffs in 15 court actions to further school desegregation in the South; 15 others to enforce fair housing laws; seven to punish denial of public accommodations to Negroes in the South; nine to penalize or terminate police and prison abuses and to require equal hiring and treatment of minority policemen; and four to enforce fair employment practices. One is moved to say: Sorry, Mr. Mitchell, but there the record is, raising hell with the Nixon-Mitchell image and the Southern Strategy.

June 12, 1971

XX

Trouble with Secrets

The first recorded comment at the White House upon the publication of the first of the documents that have come to be known as "The Pentagon Papers" was "No, we have no comment." Deputy Press Secretary Gerald Warren, who said this in answer to a question at mid-day of June 14, the day after *The New York Times* began the publication, also remarked in his only other substantive statement on the subject that the Department of Defense "has already taken action to determine the circumstances surrounding the unauthorized disclosure of classified material." A reporter's demand that Henry A. Kissinger, the assistant for national security affairs, be produced forthwith to answer questions caused Warren to say, "I am exhausted on this subject" and to defer the discussion until his superior, Press Secretary Ronald Ziegler, appeared in the press room at 1:05 P.M. But the official tone at the White House, at Defense, and at the Department of Justice had been adequately indicated with Warren's reference to "the unauthorized disclosure of classified material." Although it took several days for the fact to become fully apparent, and apparently quite a while for the controlling attitude to jell within administration councils, the desire that developed was to punish somebody for a breach of the laws and regulations governing national security. The breach could be and was excused on the grounds of First Amendment rights to free speech and free publication. But it was too obvious for denial that there had been a breach, a violation of federal regulations and probably of federal laws prohibiting the disclosure of classified documents of the kind published by the *Times* and later by other newspapers until they were temporarily estopped by the courts.

The very first desire of the President, assuming that he had made himself understood to and by his press secretary (as he usually does in important matters), was to have it known and believed that he, Mr. Nixon, neither needed nor relied upon a study ordered by the previous administration to inform him sufficiently as to the origins and problems of the Vietnam involvement. The point here was that the *Times'* Pentagon Papers consisted of original documents and conclusions drawn from them that had gone into a massive study ordered by former Defense Secretary Robert S. McNamara in 1967 and delivered to his successor, Clark Clifford, in 1968. Ronald Ziegler said that Mr. Nixon's very first order to his reorganized National Security Council was that it institute "a complete assessment and . . . interdepartmental study of the United States involvement in South Vietnam." Ziegler added that the raw memos and other documents drawn upon by the McNamara crew but not its conclusions from the documents— the McNamara study itself—were "available to the President" (really meaning, available to Henry Kissinger and his NSC staff). "The President and this administration felt it was essential to undertake our own assessment, and we did that." Before and after Nixon succeeded Lyndon Johnson, Ziegler also said, "there was a complete exchange" of information about Vietnam and Indochina policy as Nixon inherited it. Later in 1969, although Ziegler didn't mention it, there was a frantic effort extending over many weeks both to recover copies of some of the Johnson White House–NSC documents carted off to Texas and to coordinate what remained of the Johnson-time White House files with those removed to Texas. But Ziegler was probably correct in his general argument that Kissinger and others reassessing Vietnam policy for Nixon

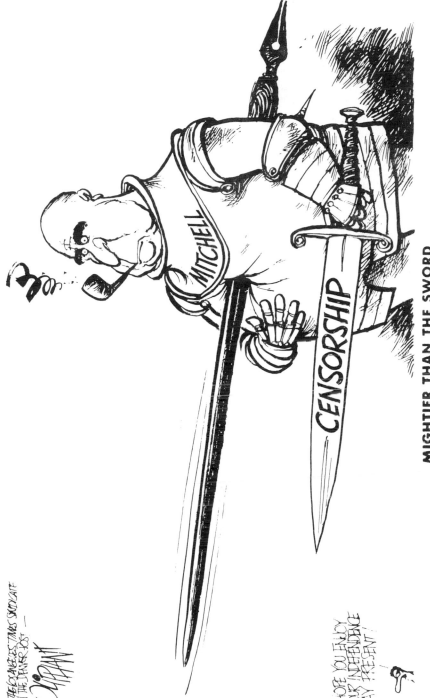

MIGHTIER THAN THE SWORD

I HOPE YOU ENJOY YOUR INDEPENDENCE DAY PRESENT!

had all the raw data from past administrations that they needed.
The Nixon policy of gradual withdrawal announced in and after
May 1969 probably would not have been importantly altered if
the new President had read every word of the McNamara study.
The same basic consideration—that US security requires a South
Vietnam free of Communist control—underlay policy in the
Johnson-McNamara time and underlies Nixon policy today.

These were the points that Ziegler wanted to get across and the
press at this stage gave him no trouble with questions of its own.
Was the President concerned about the *Times* publication? The
State Department had issued a mild expression of concern and
beyond mentioning that, Ziegler was "not going to build up, by
White House comment, the exposure of classified information."
Was Nixon angered? "I don't have a personal reaction to give
you." That afternoon and night, it turned out later, Attorney
General Mitchell first asked the *Times* to cease publication of its
"great archive" and, upon being refused, instructed the US Attorney in New York to ask a federal judge to compel the *Times* to
cease, thus beginning the series of court actions that were still
in process and appeared to be headed toward the Supreme Court
on June 24.

Question to Ziegler, June 15: "Could you tell us why the
President has ordered the Attorney General to go forward with
the harassment of *The New York Times* with subpoenas and court
orders?"

Ziegler (after disowning any "harassment"): "First of all, the
President has not ordered the Attorney General to do this. Because highly classified documents are involved here, the Secretary
of Defense requested . . . the Attorney General to conduct an
investigation of this matter. . . . As you are well aware, or at
least should be aware, there is a federal statute which spells out
very clearly the procedures relating to classified governmental
documents. Therefore, the Attorney General . . . has a responsibility to undertake an investigation and to take certain steps in
accordance with the law. That is what is being done."

The initial requests to the courts (first in New York, *in re* the
Times; then in Washington *re* the *Post*) were simply to prevent
further publication. But the Justice Department briefs and the
government attorneys' oral arguments harped with increasing and
noticeable emphasis upon the punishable violations of law and

of federal regulations that both the act of publication and the act of providing classified material to potential publishers entailed. Herbert Klein, the President's Director of Communications, told a select group of Washington correspondents that Mr. Nixon's predominant concern was not any harm that *this* publication might do but the harm to the presidency as an institution that uninhibited and (Klein implied) unpunished dissemination and publication of classified information might do. Ziegler, pressed as to whether Mr. Nixon had been consulted about and had specifically approved the legal moves to prevent publication, said that both Nixon and Mitchell had told him that the President "accepted" his Attorney General's judgment that in the situation created by the *Times* the government should not and "would not waive its responsibility to carry out the law."

By June 19, Ziegler was emphasizing for the first time the assertion that the President himself has "a responsibility . . . to enforce the law of the land" in respect to "what is considered to be unauthorized handling of highly classified documents." A continuing question, more often left unspoken than spoken at White House press sessions, was why the Nixon administration didn't let documents and analytic conclusions from those documents that dealt with and reflected upon the previous administrations speak for themselves. Ziegler answered for Nixon: "The decisions and the policies developed in the previous administration are beside the point, as far as we are concerned. The point is that we have a responsibility to enforce the law when there is unauthorized handling and disclosure of information which is specifically prohibited by law."

Why, then, didn't the Administration proceed to criminal prosecution? District Attorney Whitney North Seymour said in New York that prosecution would be likely to expose and emphasize the accuracy of the disclosed information. Mr. Nixon may have given another piece of the answer when he promised to let Congress have the Pentagon Papers—still under security wraps, of course, but in circumstances that appeared to guarantee *authorized* publication later on.

July 3, 1971

———

The Administration lost its effort to prevent newspaper publication of the Pentagon Papers. It published its own version in a Government Printing Office set of 12 volumes, and, in Boston and Los Angeles federal courts, relentlessly pursued its efforts to try and convict those whom it held responsible for the original leak—chiefly Daniel Ellsberg, a former Defense researcher, and *Times* reporter Neil Sheehan.

XXI

Showdown with Reagan

At the Department of Health, Education, and Welfare, one of the two federal agencies where Mr. Nixon's problems with Governor Ronald Reagan of California are centered, the impression is that there isn't any problem any more. Reagan's arrogant demands for the waiver of federal welfare standards and the President's disgraceful show of surrender to those demands appear to have died with the demise of the governor's state welfare proposals in his own legislature in Sacramento. Two strong administrators, Secretary Elliot Richardson and Under Secretary John Veneman, a sometime California legislator who is blessed with an acute appreciation of Reagan's capacity for bluffing, seem to have waited him out and to have demonstrated to their masters at the White House that the governor has lost so much standing and credence in California that he is in no position to be the threat to Mr. Nixon's renomination and reelection next year that he was assumed to be back in March and April. The remaining welfare issues, having mostly to do with token payments for federally subsidized medical care for the poor and with a diminished requirement that employable welfare beneficiaries work at available jobs, are in line with the President's national welfare proposals and will not, when and if they are finally approved, call for any serious abandonment of federal decency.

At the other agency, the Office of Economic Opportunity, the situation and the indications of White House attitudes toward Reagan to be drawn from it are very different. An OEO decision last week, bearing importantly upon the future of federally provided legal assistance for the poor in California and the nation, appears on its face to indicate that the President is still as afraid of Governor Reagan's potential for trouble in 1972 as Mr. Nixon seemed to be last spring and that he is still prepared to go to any conceivable lengths to pay off Reagan with whatever Reagan wants. It *appears*—the word must be emphasized, for reasons to be explained shortly—to indicate that the President and his advisers share the opinion of a good many politicians, among them some of Reagan's Democratic detractors, that his prospective leadership of the California delegation at the Republican convention in 1972 and his continuing national appeal to conservative voters could, if events generally are not going well for Mr. Nixon, outweigh the governor's decline in California itself and make him a substantial and hostile factor both at the convention and in the election campaign. Therefore, according to this reasoning, the President must as a matter of sheer precaution take care whenever possible to placate Reagan and to take special care in matters that concern the governor.

One of those matters, perhaps the one that concerns Reagan more than any other, is OEO's Legal Services program. The biggest of 37 OEO legal programs in California is California Rural Legal Assistance, Inc. Its 44 lawyers, directed from CRLA headquarters in San Francisco, serve the poor in nine California counties. CRLA has angered Reagan with a series of successful "class actions" in state and federal courts that have forced his administration to end or at least mitigate abuses in fields ranging from medical care to the provision of food stamps and fair treatment of Mexican-American children in public schools. OEO Director Frank Carlucci, a borrowed Foreign Service Officer who means well but clearly should return to foreign diplomacy, upheld Reagan's veto last January of a grant of $1.8 million to CRLA for 1971 and, in an outrageous evasion dictated for the President by John D. Ehrlichman, the White House assistant for domestic affairs, substituted a conditional six-month grant that expires July 31. Reagan professed to be "very pleased and gratified," as he should have been, by the accompanying and gratuitous reflections upon a program that had been praised by five successive teams of federal evaluators. Reagan based his veto upon 135 charges against CRLA, manufactured for him by his State Office of Economic Opportunity, a federally funded front whose director, Lewis K. Uhler, has just been accused in a civil suit of misusing $100,000 of federal money. Carlucci dignified the Reagan-Uhler charges by, among others things, referring them to the Justice Department and the Civil Service Commission for "possible violations of federal law or federal prohibitions on political activity" by CRLA lawyers. Carlucci never announced that Justice and the commission found no evidence to support the charges.

Carlucci also appointed "a high-level commission" to conduct "a full and impartial review of the matter" and to guide him in deciding whether to fund CRLA after July 31. That commission, headed by retired Chief Justice Robert B. Williamson of Maine, conducted hearings in California and submitted its findings to Carlucci on June 25. At Reagan's order, Uhler and his State OEO refused to participate in the hearings beyond submitting the Uhler charges and (in the commission's words) "some 3000 pages of exhibits purporting to document the factual allegations." The commission summarized its 400-page report as follows: "Based upon the record before it, consisting of the voluminous testimony of 165 witnesses at 20 days of public hearings . . . the Commission finds and concludes . . . that CRLA has been discharging its duty to provide legal assistance to the poor . . . in a highly competent, efficient and exemplary manner. We, therefore, recommend that California Rural Legal Assistance, Inc., be continued and refunded." The commission noted "occasional instances of lapses in administrative supervision and control of sometimes young and inexperienced attorneys" and "isolated instances of a lack of judgment" that had contributed to "misunderstanding" and criticism of CRLA. But it said that these instances "are not of any great magnitude" and that the major Reagan-Uhler charges "were totally irresponsible and without foundation."

Carlucci, announcing his decision to refund CRLA on June 30, did not quote a single line of the commission's positive findings. The most that he brought himself to attribute to the commission was, in his paraphrase, a finding that "on the whole CRLA has provided a useful service to the rural poor" of California. Although the commission had disavowed any concern with the general issues involved in legal assistance, he said the commission report "forced" him "to the conclusion that many significant issues of public policy have been raised by Governor Reagan." Carlucci concluded his announcement with a confession that: "This decision . . . has been discussed with Governor Reagan, who has advised me of his concurrence."

The essence of Carlucci's decision had been determined long before he received the commission report. It was checked at every stage with John Ehrlichman at the White House but not, I was told there and am inclined to believe, dictated to the extent that the January decision was. It didn't have to be. The main lines of Nixon policy on legal aid for the poor, in California and elsewhere, were determined in April and set forth in a presidential message to Congress on May 5, proposing that the entire federal legal aid program be transferred from OEO to a theoretically independent and federally funded Legal Services Corporation. It can be argued that this would be a more effective instrument than OEO's directly administered system has proven to be. The President's primary purpose, connected with but by no means confined to his Reagan problem, is defined with utter frankness at the White House. The purpose is to get off the President's back the political problems that are bound to arise from any publicly financed legal aid program for which his administration is directly responsible. Carlucci was required to serve that purpose with his California decision, and it can be understood only in this light.

CRLA applied for a grant of $2.65 million that would see it through the 17 months from July 31 to the end of 1972. Carlucci promised in his statement to approve a 17-month grant, "subject to 22 special conditions" and to yet another reevaluation of CRLA performance before the money for 1972 is released. His statement said that OEO, Reagan's state government and the California Bar Association would do the reevaluating. He also promised to approve a special grant of $2.5 million to finance an experimental study and then a 12-month trial of federally financed legal assistance to be provided by private attorneys and local bar associations. It was all very curious, very obscure and highly conditional. But, in the declared opinion of CRLA Director Cruz Reynoso and of several dedicated friends of genuine legal aid for the poor, the decision was not necessarily the equivocal cheat that it could be interpreted to be. Carlucci has promised that the next evaluators will include responsible representatives of the American Bar Association, among others, and will not be dominated by Reagan foes of CRLA. He has also indicated to Reynoso and other CRLA advocates that the imposed "conditions" will amount to no more than restrictions that CRLA already observes. That is not Ronald Reagan's understanding. He said he was "delighted," and he still has the power to veto the actual grant. It could be, and I hope it is, Governor Reagan who has been cheated.

July 10, 1971

Reagan let the provisional 1971 grant stand without the promised reevaluation and seemed willing later to await the absorption of CRLA in a nation-wide Legal Services Corporation.

XXII

China Gamble

The name of the game was the trip itself. Kissinger in Peking and afterward at San Clemente and in Washington, and the President, announcing that Kissinger had been to Communist China's capital and that he had "accepted with pleasure" an invitation to go there before next May 1, framed the great adventure in terms that excluded any need for a showing of such concrete results as hastened peace in Vietnam or the immediate diplomatic recognition of the People's Republic of China by the United States in order to make the Nixon visit appear to have been an historic success. Mr. Nixon ordered his Cabinet and begged congressional leaders of both parties to avoid and discourage speculation that might enhance the instant euphoria and the general expectation of world-shaking results that followed the President's televised announcement.

The last ounce of politically useful drama was extracted from the disclosure and from the secrecy that veiled Kissinger's preparatory visit. Once that was accomplished, however, the effort at the

White House and at the State Department was to project the President's forthcoming journey to the Peking summit as a self-fulfilling endeavor "to promote better relations in the world and thereby to contribute to the peace of all nations." Scorn was thrown upon the notion that "some hot deal," some gimmicky arrangement with the Peking government, necessarily had to flow from the President's trip if it was not to end with "a sense of failure." Premier Chou En-lai cooperated in Peking. In his first published comments after the Kissinger visit, to a group of visiting American scholars, he emphasized the importance to the People's Republic and to the world of the Communist invitation and of the President's acceptance. The later statement of a lesser Communist official, Central Committeeman Kuo Mo-jo, that Mr. Nixon has to show "some results" beforehand if he "really wants to come to China" was dismissed in Washington as the expected vaporings of a negligible figure.

The amazing thing is that the world, so much of its press and so many of its governments were amazed. Seldom and maybe never has a major turn in American foreign policy been so thoroughly signaled in advance. Mr. Nixon's personal ambition to be the President who brought the US and Communist China into accord dates from 1967, when he wrote of the need for such a policy in *Foreign Affairs*. We of the White House press corps were told by our favorite presidential briefer last December 24, during a year-end review of foreign policy, that this administration was ready and anxious to resume talks with the Chinese Communists "at Warsaw *or elsewhere.*" Edgar Snow reported in the April 30 *Life* that Chairman Mao had said Mr. Nixon would be welcomed in China. Snow also wrote that Washington, in February, had just conveyed to Peking the latest of several offers to send an intermediary to arrange a Nixon visit. The President has been saying since April that he hoped and expected to visit Communist China "in some capacity." He publicly recognized on April 29 "a significant change" at the United Nations in the previous resistance to the Peking government's admission to that body and support for the Taiwan government's continued status in it as the China member. Consultations with other governments, including the Taiwan and Japanese governments, on the pending abandonment of US opposition to Peking's admission to the UN, have been going on for months. I reported in this journal's May 1 issue

'—THEN, WHEN HE GETS RIGHT UP TO THE GATE . . .'

that Henry Kissinger, at the President's order, had been working since the Nixon administration's earliest days to establish effective and friendly communication with Peking and that the Administration was ready for serious business whenever Peking was ready. The announced schedule of Kissinger's "fact-finding trip" to Asia and Paris was so vague and loose that any fool (I have myself particularly in mind) should have perceived, with all of the recent background at hand, that his main destination was Peking. Yet we of the press and, it now turns out, the highest officials of immediately interested governments, notably those in Taiwan and Tokyo, were simply not prepared to believe that *this* President, this man who had made a career of forceful anticommunism, was actually capable of so drastic and dramatic a break not only with past American policy but with his own pattern of attitude and behavior. More important aspects aside, it all provides a lesson in the folly of stereotyping Richard Nixon.

What comes next is what matters. Dependable information upon that score was very sparse after Kissinger reported to the President in California and they returned to the White House. At a press briefing in California (a reporter at a White House press session put on the public record the fact that it was "a Kissinger briefing"), and at a later one Kissinger gave a few journalists (this writer not included) in Washington, he resolutely refused to discuss the substance of his talks with Chou En-lai. He confined himself to trivia that did nothing to minimize his role and the enormous impression that Chou and the other Chinese Communists he met made upon him. But some facts as to what had passed with the Peking officials and what the administration now expects did emerge in Washington.

Kissinger in Peking informally accepted the invitation to the President only after Chou and the other Communist conferees, who did not include Mao Tse-tung, convinced him that no foreseeable difference between the two governments would bring about cancellation of the invitation after Mr. Nixon had formally accepted it. Chou convinced Kissinger, and Kissinger convinced Chou, that the Nixon visit in itself, results apart, was in the national interests of both governments and that, once the invitation and acceptance had been announced, *nothing* should be allowed to obstruct the Nixon trip or let it end with "a sense of failure." When I remarked to an American official that nothing short of

war between Communist China and the US could prevent the
President's journey or impede a mutual claim of immense success
after it occurred, he grinned rather feebly and said that was a
fair conclusion.

One of the major points of mutual interest identified and agreed
upon in Peking was that Communist China should participate in
a final settlement of the whole Indochina problem, at an international conference of the kind proposed by Mr. Nixon last
October. The grim appearance of continuing failure in Paris to
negotiate a settlement of the Vietnam conflict notwithstanding, the
hope and expectation in both Peking and Washington is that at
least the beginnings of a Vietnam settlement will be negotiated
this year, before Nixon goes to Peking, on terms that will contribute to a later settlement applying to Laos and Cambodia too.

What he heard from Kissinger satisfied Chou En-lai that Mr.
Nixon had indeed abandoned US resistance to Peking's admission
to UN as *the* China member and that this government's obligations
to the rival Taiwan government of Chiang Kai-shek would not be
allowed to obstruct the outcome in September. Chiang has been
told that the US will fight for the retention of a seat for Taiwan
only in the General Assembly and will do that much only if
Chiang demands it. His refusal up to July 28 to reply to this
communication complicated the difficulties of devising a satisfac-
tory announcement of the new US position, a chore the President
gladly left to Secretary of State Rogers. Whether Peking accepts
or rejects a UN seat on two-China terms, and Chiang does the
same, is in a sense incidental to the US government. Either outcome, it is figured, would remove the Taiwan issue as an obstruction to improved relationships with Peking and, from the
Communist Chinese standpoint, would lessen if not eliminate the
onus the US bears for its diminished support of Taiwan in or out
of the UN.

An unforeseen aftermath of the Nixon announcement was its
impact upon the Japanese government. Japan's Taiwan ties are
close, its interests there are large, and its government's sense of
obligation to the Taiwan government turns out to be a good deal
deeper and more compelling than Mr. Nixon's. Working out the
resultant difficulties with Japan, which is intended to be "a corner-
stone" of the changing US posture in Asia, preoccupied the White

House and State Department in July more than the Taiwan problem did.

August 7 and 14, 1971

───────

After the UN admitted the People's Republic and expelled the Taiwan government in October, Mr. Nixon appeared to be considerably less displeased with the result than he was with the raucous glee with which some of the smaller country delegations greeted the action. On November 12, announcing his intention to withdraw an additional 45,000 troops from Vietnam in December and January, the President placed great emphasis upon his continuing desire to negotiate an Indochina-wide ceasefire.

XXIII

Austin Story

The intent of this report is to summarize the factors that led Mr. Nixon to make his August 3 statement on school desegregation and busing. In my opinion, the statement marked the low point of the Nixon presidency to date. It cloaked a decent and necessary action, the appeal of a federal district judge's decision in a symbolic school case in Austin, Texas, in the misleading semantics of opposition to busing "to achieve a racial balance" and "for the sake of busing" with which Mr. Nixon has been deceiving his white southern constituency and the entire country since 1968. It taught me never again to assume, as I did in two recent pieces about Nixon school policy, that the President is capable of acting or of letting his subordinates act in good faith on desegregation. The politics of the issue are simply too much for Mr. Nixon and for whatever sense of public integrity he may retain. Once that is said, there is no point in further denunciation. The President responded in the statement to very real pressures and to what he took to be signs of some important changes in the nation's racial attitudes as they are reflected in the public schools. The story behind the response, as it is disclosed in fragments by officials who are under strict instructions to keep quiet, is incomplete and tainted with more than a touch of the paranoia that is increasingly evident at and near the Nixon White House. But, to the extent that it is known, the story is worth telling.

It was unfortunate for all concerned, most of all for Mr. Nixon, that an accident of timing made the Austin case the occasion for the Administration's first and token reaction to the Supreme Court's historic *Swann* decision of April 20. With fateful results throughout the South and, in the end, throughout the country, that decision was widely reported and understood to require massive busing of students to public schools outside their neighborhoods in cities and towns where traces of racial segregation once imposed by law still remained. In fact, the Supreme Court said only that busing is "a normal and accepted tool of educational policy" and that lower courts *may* require more of it when in their judgment more busing is necessary in order to eliminate remnants of "legally imposed school segregation." The common and inaccurately extreme interpretation had a shock effect everywhere in the South, the capital city of Texas included. It stiffened segregationist resistance, inflated the hopes and demands of all-out integrationists, and generally eroded the attitude of resigned acceptance among white southerners that had accounted in substantial part for the considerable progress in school desegregation achieved in 1970–71. The effects were becoming dimly apparent when, in May, the Nixon administration had to put up or shut up in the Austin case. They hit the administration officials handling school desegregation, at the White House and at the Departments of Justice and Health, Education, and Welfare, with full force in June and July, and the impression then conveyed to Mr. Nixon powerfully influenced the stance he took in August. He came to feel that in the immediate aftermath and heat of *Swann* he had been led by two of his trusted Cabinet members, Attorney General Mitchell and HEW Secretary Richardson, and by some of his White House assistants to approve in essence if not in detail a federal desegregation plan for the Austin schools that not only ignored changing realities but may have gone beyond what the Supreme Court actually required in the way of inter-school and cross-city busing.

Both the demographic and the political complexities of the

Austin situation compounded this impression. Austin is a tri-cultural city of white "Anglos," Mexican-Americans and blacks. Its desegregation problem is not, therefore, the black-white prob-lem characteristic of the South. Some 23 percent of its public school students are Mexican-Americans, only 16 percent are black. Most of its students attend schools that are predominantly and respectively white, Mexican-American and black. But the state and city authorities have never segregated the Mexican-Americans by law, as they segregated the blacks until 1955. In undertaking the complete desegregation of all Austin schools, as HEW and Justice did with the plan submitted to Federal District Judge Jack Roberts on May 14, the Administration took on all the burdens and diffi-culties of what federal attorneys call "a northern situation," in which a history of segregation by covert design rather than by open law has to be proved. Neither Judge Roberts nor the Austin school authorities questioned the federal contention that illegal remnants of black segregation persist. The only argument on that count was and still is over the amount of busing and other remedial measures required to eliminate the remnants. My reading of the federal brief and a skim of the trial record suggest to me that Joseph Rich, the Justice attorney assigned to the case, proved that Austin's Mexican-Americans have been deliberately segregated, too. On the facts before him, however, Judge Roberts ruled that Austin Chicanos are not and never have been illegally segregated in the schools. A feeling that it was hopeless to appeal this part of the Roberts decision was evident afterward among HEW and Justice officials and attorneys. Mr. Nixon presumably had this view in mind when he said in his statement that the appeal he approved was being taken to the Fifth Circuit Court "on limited constitu-tional grounds." The Washington consensus was that if the circuit's appellate judges, probably the country's busiest with desegregation cases, choose to reinstate the Mexican-American issue, well and good. Otherwise, the issue will have been reduced to the relatively simple problem of desegregating black schools and the amount of additional busing required will have been correspondingly reduced.

Whether the political complexities exist only in the minds and suspicions of Nixon officials is a question I can't answer. That they exist there, I have no doubt. The suspicions are rooted in the following facts. Will Davis, the president of the Austin district school board, is an active Democrat and a former chairman of the

Texas Democratic executive committee. Judge Roberts is also a Democrat, a Lyndon Johnson appointee to the federal bench, and a friend of Will Davis. With a tenacity that is rare nowadays among local school authorities in the traditional Deep South, the Davis board has clung to a plan for limited and part-time desegregation that would, even in the favorable opinion of Judge Roberts, do no more than bring about intermittent interracial association in Austin's white and black elementary schools "as much as 25 percent" of the school year. During a long and embittered huddle with HEW and Justice officials in Washington, after the administration plan was submitted, Davis displayed what seemed to his antagonists to be utter confidence in the ultimate decision of Judge Roberts. It is said at the White House that Treasury Secretary John Connally, Mr. Nixon's temporarily captive Democrat from Texas, tried at the President's request and failed to persuade Davis to concede enough to make the local plan acceptable to HEW and Justice. The resultant suspicion was voiced to me at the White House and was imparted to the President. It was that Judge Roberts and his friend Davis were in cahoots all along to produce a local plan and a lower court decision that the Administration would be compelled to reject and appeal despite the predictable and, in the event, adverse political effects.

Other factors entered. One of them was a sudden eruption of anti-busing sentiment and apprehension in Congress, climaxed with a House vote in favor of a restrictive and politically menacing amendment to the President's Emergency School Assistance Act. Another disturbing element was reported in detail to Secretary Richardson by his civil rights director, Stanley Pottinger, in a summary of the circumstances that led to and complicated the Austin problem. Its thrust was that a growing number of black community leaders and of the attorneys who represent the black interest in desegregation cases were losing their old passion for the degree and kinds of desegregation presumed to be required by the Supreme Court and hitherto sought by HEW and Justice. If this were true, it raised the horrifying possibility that Mr. Nixon had let himself be shoved out ahead not only of his white constituency in the South and elsewhere but of the sentiment in portions of the black community. The evidence adduced was thin, but it was enough to shake the confidence of Richardson and

Attorney General Mitchell in the soundness of their previous positions and advice to Mr. Nixon.

Thus it was that Secretary Richardson accepted in silence and loyalty, though with private sorrow, the harsh language in which the President said he would have the Justice Department "disavow" the Austin plan. Mitchell used much milder language in his own announcement and otherwise remained totally uncommunicative. He had reason to be reticent: he no less than Elliot Richardson was "repudiated," as the press put it, by the President's statement, for he had reviewed and cleared the disavowed Austin plan. As for the President's resort to the deceptive semantics of anti-busing, nothing remains to be said except that he had a purpose in it apart from his obvious desire to minimize the political penalties of the court appeal. He was saying once more to every subordinate concerned with the issue, including Cabinet members and his own assistants, that he damn well expected his limited concept of desegregation and attendant busing to prevail and would tolerate no deviations from it. He wanted no official action that would expose the falsity of his pretense to be simultaneously "against busing" and for desegregation.

August 21 and 28, 1971

XXIV

Turnabout

The story peddled last week at the White House and at the Treasury Department next door was that the only sudden thing about the reversal of domestic and international economic policy announced by Mr. Nixon on August 15 was the announcement itself. His counsellors and spokesmen went to great lengths, publicly and in private, to squelch any notion that the President acted in panic and without the long and careful forethought that he always likes to have attributed to him. For the most part and remarkably enough, considering the Nixon administration's aptitude for calculated deceit, the known record bears out the official story. It shows that Mr. Nixon was feeling his way for many months, certainly since last May and perhaps since last November, toward his 90-day freeze on wages, prices and rents. His suspension of the dollar's last ties to gold, his imposition of a surcharge on imports, and his proposals to reduce taxes and budgeted expenditures were of later origin, but they were considered in June and some of them were forecast by one of his economic advisers,

Herbert Stein, in mid-July. The President finally decided to do
and propose all of these things in the 48 hours before he announced them on television. It appears to be true that he decided
to announce them then because of the signs, evident through the
preceding week on the international money markets, that much
of the world was on the verge of a catastrophic loss of confidence
in the United States dollar. It also appears to be true within limits
that the monetary crisis was only the catalyst, the immediate
occasion, for decisions that had been, as Treasury Secretary John
B. Connally said, "long in the making."

The biggest domestic decision had been long in the making,
that is, if one year to the day can be said to be a long time in
the evolution of policy. On August 15, 1970, Mr. Nixon signed
the act of Congress that gave him the authority to impose his
wage-price freeze. He recalled then that "I have previously indicated that I did not intend to exercise such authority if it were
given to me," and added, "Price and wage controls simply do
not fit the conditions which exist today." If Congress believed
that price and wage controls were needed, he said, "it should face
up to its responsibilities and make such controls mandatory." In
retrospect, the meaningful fact is that he approved a law which
he said he didn't want. Its sweeping grant of power occurs in
these words: "The President is authorized to issue such orders
and regulations as he may deem appropriate to stabilize prices,
rents, wages and salaries at levels not less than those prevailing
on May 25, 1970." Within three months of the signing, in November, he was telling his economic advisers that if he ever did
intervene to control wages and prices he would go all the way,
to an absolute freeze rather than to variable controls that would
require detailed policing. In March 1971 he used the authority
for the first time, to impose a timid semblance of wage controls
upon the construction industry and its rapacious unions. In April,
through subordinates, he begged Congress to let him keep the
power for two years after it was to expire on May 31.
    That request brought into the open a new conflict of view and
sharpened an old one between the President and his first White
House Counsellor, Chairman Arthur Burns of the Federal Reserve
Board. Burns objected that a prolonged extension "would give

COMES THE THAW . . . .

the President virtually dictatorial power. If the Congress gives the President this kind of power, it ought to review it at brief intervals." Six months was the longest the President should have it, three months was preferable and two weeks would be ideal, Burns told a Senate committee. Treasury Under Secretary Charles Walker, speaking for Nixon, argued strongly that an unqualified two-year extension would be "in the public interest" and said it was "highly unlikely" that the President would use "the general powers" without asking Congress for "a further specific mandate." Congress, expecting but not requiring a chance to grant a further mandate, extended the wage-price authority to April 30, 1972. Nixon, who had issued a written statement of his objections to the 1970 law, let his press staff announce orally and with minimal emphasis his approval of the extension on May 18. He and his senior assistants noted without comment that Burns at the same Senate hearings had said he "definitely" favored the kind of national wage-price review board, to establish guidelines and encourage voluntary compliance with them, that the President opposed. Burns did not then or later advocate mandatory controls. But he continued to irritate the men around Nixon with his insistence that the President use his "great moral authority" to discourage inflationary increases, and his expressed doubts that existing Nixon policies were enough to break the inflationary spiral.

Nixon during this period maintained, and had his spokesmen maintain, that his economic policies of fiscal expansion through swelling budget deficits and the least possible interference with market processes were slowly but surely bringing down the rates of inflation and unemployment. There was in these assertions a subdued promise of change, of more positive action, if milder policies failed to accomplish the desired results. "This is an activist administration," he said on May 1. If he concluded that "this economy is not moving as fast as it should move to deal with the unemployment problem, then we will act. We will act on the tax and other fronts." His advisers pointed last week to that statement and to subsequent ones like it as evidence, clear to some of his associates but not to the public when the statements were made, that the President between May and mid-July was moving steadily toward the admission and decision that a great deal more than he was doing had to be done if declines in the key economic indexes were to be halted and the occasional gains were to be improved upon. His new Secretary of the Treasury, John Connally, did nothing after August 15 to discourage the widely believed story that he had been urging the President toward more positive action ever since he joined the Cabinet in February. No doubt he had been. But conversations at the White House suggest that Big John and his friends may have been overdoing the inflation of Connally and the accompanying deflation of such advisers as George Shultz, the director of the Office of Management and Budget, and Paul McCracken, the chairman of the Council of Economic Advisers. It was true that they had personified and expounded policies that the President reversed. But they took their medicine in gentlemanly quiet, they did not oppose to the point of either public or private obstruction the course announced on the 15th, and they displayed the sort of disciplined acceptance and loyalty that Mr. Nixon in the long run tends to value above more flamboyant talents.

At a suddenly convened press conference on August 4, Mr. Nixon did two things that lend credibility to the hindsight accounts that he by then had decided everything but the timing and some details of the moves he announced 11 days later. He indicated for the first time that he just might consider the establishment of a federal wage and price review board, a device that he had consistently scorned in the past. And he made public amends to Arthur Burns, whose cooperation with any new course of national and international action would be essential, for a nasty story that had been leaked from the White House to the press the previous week. The story was that Burns, the stern advocate of austerity, had begged the President for a $20,000 raise in his $42,500 salary and that Mr. Nixon was thinking of asking Congress to put the independent FRB under his direct control. Not so, said Mr. Nixon, leaving the false impression that journalists and not somebody on his own staff had taken what he called "a cheap shot" at Burns. The President said that he and Burns were then and always had been in agreement on the big issues and did his (in the circumstances) rather noxious best to allay frictions that in truth had marred the relationship since late 1969. It worked, in the sense that Arthur Burns was among those who led the official applause for the new course.

What next? Here I take as gospel the word of John Connally that it won't be a return to the passive stance that prevailed before

August 15. He was entitled to belief when he said: "I think the President is prepared to take whatever action is necessary to maintain a stable economy in this country."

September 4, 1971

XXV

Truth and Busing

In the four weeks since Mr. Nixon chose in early August to say once more that he is "against busing as that term is commonly used in school desegregation cases" and that he had ordered his Attorney General and his Secretary of Health, Education, and Welfare to hold federally imposed busing "to the minimum required by law," the job of explaining to gullible voters and politicians in the South and elsewhere that the President didn't really mean what they were led to think he meant has been pretty well completed. They were led to think that he as President had the power and was going to use his power to halt the nationwide increase in the busing of students in biracial and multiracial towns and cities from their neighborhoods to public schools in other neighborhoods. Federal officials in Washington and throughout the land have been explaining since then, though not of course in the terms used here, that the President is neither the liar nor the ignoramus that a strict construction of his August statement might make him out to be. It is being said for him that he understood in August, as he understood when he spoke to the same effect and manufactured the same impression during his 1968 campaign for election, that "the minimum required by law" is a lot of busing and that he in fact could neither put a stop to extensive busing nor substantially reduce the required amount of it. All he meant to say, the explanation goes, was that he doesn't like busing and is sorry that Congress and the courts have required him to countenance and enforce so much of it. People who understood him to be saying a great deal more than that have been reminded of their duty to comprehend that politics is politics and that when the President speaks as a politician working his way toward reelection in 1972 he expects that the fine distinction between literal truth and customary deception will be recognized.

The opening of the 1971–72 school year demonstrated that the evolution of desegregation law and the expanding role of the courts in defining it have indeed reduced the relative power of the President and of federal agencies to determine the extent of the busing and other remedial measures deemed necessary in order to end racial and ethnic segregation in the public schools. More and not less busing, the President's sentiments notwithstanding, turned out to be the rule in most of the South and in some hitherto unaffected cities in other sections. Aside from whatever political good his August statement may have done him, and the amount of good it did him is subject to doubt, the principal effect was upon the bureaucracies in HEW and the Department of Justice. They got the Nixon message, reenforced with a later White House warning that officials who didn't get it could find themselves in some other line of work, that in drafting school compliance plans and expounding administration policy in the federal courts, they were expected by the President to adopt and adhere to a modest estimate of "the minimum required by law." Since the officials concerned thought they were doing that all along, the actual difference in practice was fairly small. It was more a difference in attitude than in the requirements finally laid upon school districts. Federal enthusiasm for desegregation as a socially desirable objective was out. The utmost caution in attaining it was in. The recommended posture in dealing with local school boards, outraged parents and offended politicians was to seem to be as sorry as the President professed to be that anything at all had to be done to satisfy the law and the Constitution as they were interpreted by the courts.

One of the officials who understood the revised requirements and showed great aplomb in complying with them was J. Stanley Pottinger, director of HEW's Office for Civil Rights. He acknowledged that his staff and the Justice Department lawyers working with him may have overestimated the busing and other requirements that the Supreme Court had originally been thought to proclaim in a landmark decision on April 20. He let some Southern school districts (Wayne County, NC, for one) get away for the time-being with limited desegregation plans that he would have rejected in July. He dutifully admonished his regional directors in the South and elsewhere to keep in mind that "the minimum required by law" could be even less than local school authorities in some districts had offered to do about desegregation until the word got around that the President was doing the little he could to lower the Administration's standards. Pottinger also noted and took quiet advantage of an interesting and superficially contradictory change in the attitude of Attorney General John Mitchell. In 1969 and through much of 1970, Mitchell had restrained HEW's use of its statutory power to deny federal funds to school districts that refused to meet the desegregation standards then prevailing. His theory was that it was politically wiser to let the courts bear the main burden of enforcement. Now that tactic was playing out, with the spreading realization that the courts generally ordered into effect compliance plans that HEW had devised and the Justice Department had defended. Mitchell remarked in mid-August that maybe it was time to resume use of the cut-off power, and Pottinger proceeded or prepared to do it in several pending cases. It normally takes longer to complete the administrative procedures that must precede a final cut-off than it does to get effective court orders, and there was some suspicion that the Administration had merely hit upon another way to delay action. But, at a time when the whole emphasis appeared to be upon minimizing desegregation, a valuable tool of enforcement had been restored to use. It was one of several indications that there was more pretense than actuality in the amended Nixon posture of opposition to extensive busing.

The first 1971–72 emergency grants to school districts in the throes of desegregation were announced on August 27. Forty-one districts in 14 states, among them seven non-Southern states, re-

'OF COURSE, THIS FORCED BUSING IS ONLY A TEMPORARY MEASURE WHILE WE LEARN TO LOVE ONE ANOTHER, OR SOMETHING . . .'

ceived $22.5 million of the $62 million available for the new
school year. The balance had to be allocated by September 10,
when HEW's temporary authority to help districts meet the costs
of desegregation was to expire. The authority will be renewed only
if Congress stops diddling with the Administration's $1.5 billion
Emergency School Assistance Act and passes one of the pending
versions of it. About $2 million of $75 million appropriated for
interim desegregation assistance in 1970–71 went for the additional
busing that any large increase in urban desegregation inevitably
demands. The $110 million requested by this year's 41 initial
grantees and chopped down by HEW's Office of Education included about $10 million for busing. In accordance with Mr.
Nixon's promise that no more federal money will be used for
busing, not a penny of the $22.5 million was allowed for that
purpose. Herman R. Goldberg, the Associate Commissioner of
Education in charge of the program, assured the applicants that
this was a good thing, not because the President had ordered it
but because the money might better be used to improve the education offered at the end of the bus rides. Some of the deprived
officials must have had a wry laugh when they compared this argument with the scoring system used to determine eligibility for the
emergency funds. Two of the major criteria were the number of
students to be shifted from schools they would ordinarily attend
to other schools, and the ratio of this number to the district's total
school enrollment. Districts with the largest numbers and propor-
tions of transferred students got most of the money. Districts that
proposed little or no student transfer for desegregation got little
or none. This was logical, since the purpose of the grants was to
ease and further desegregation. But it constituted one more commentary upon the fallacy of Mr. Nixon's claim to be "against
busing."

Commissioner Goldberg also oversees what's left of HEW's staff
effort in what used to be called "civil rights education," meaning
in large part the monitoring of local compliance with desegregation
law and the drafting of compliance plans. The staffers who did this
work irritated many white Southerners with politically damaging
effects. Very little of the function is left, the policy now being to
take HEW out of that business and use federally paid consultants.
Budget authority to do that much expires with the emergency grant

authority, and HEW must soon ask Congress for money to keep its Division of Equal Educational Opportunity alive.

September 11, 1971

————

HEW's educational opportunity division remained alive, though just barely, while Congress postponed action on the Emergency School Assistance Act until 1972.

XXVI

Praggy Dick

The favored descriptive of Mr. Nixon at the White House these days is "pragmatic." One imagines his chief assistants drooling with pleasure when James Reston and other commentators perceive in the President's turns toward Communist China and away from the principles of a free economy the creative pragmatism that his associates and spokesmen declare to be his central and greatest virtue. At long last, his official apologists are saying, the basic characteristic of Richard Nixon and of the Nixon presidency is being recognized and accorded its due.

The psalmists of Nixon pragmatism wouldn't jibe at applying to the President and his current performance the Random House Dictionary's definitions of the terms they use: "Pragmatism: . . . a philosophical movement or system stressing practical consequences and values by which concepts are to be analyzed and their validity determined"; and "Pragmatist: one who is oriented toward the success or failure of a given line of action, thought, etc.; a practical person." Some discomfort is manifested when the

inference that Mr. Nixon doesn't believe in anything is drawn.
That, the inquirer is told, is the wrong way to put it. The right
(or preferred) way to put it is that Mr. Nixon doesn't let his beliefs, which are said to be deep and strong, debar him from any
line of action that seems to him to be necessary and practical,
however inconsistent it may appear to be with prior lines of action
and profession. There is an important difference, it is said for
Mr. Nixon, between a lack of commitment and a constructive
freedom from commitment. The President, it is further said, enjoys
a freedom from commitment that enables him to deal with circumstances as he finds them and in consequence to be a resourceful
and effective President. The general response to his freeze of wages
and prices, a move that contradicted every rule of government and
economics that he had previously advocated, and the paralyzing
frustration that his steps toward accommodation with Communist
China inflicted upon his liberal critics, are cited in evidence that
Nixon pragmatism works and pays.

A pragmatic President needs pragmatic assistants. "You'll notice," a Nixon pragmatist remarked with merry satisfaction, "that
all of our ideologues are gone." He mentioned Daniel Patrick
Moynihan, a liberal Democrat who returned to the Harvard faculty
in early 1971, and Arthur Burns, a conservative economist and
sometime White House Counsellor who was elevated to the Federal Reserve Board chairmanship in early 1970. Their departures,
it seemed to the surviving assistant, had lessened tensions and improved the team spirit at the White House. Moynihan never let
his liberalism get out of hand during his two years on the Nixon
staff: he was offered and declined the American ambassadorship
to the UN; and he has just been appointed to the delegation at
this year's General Assembly session. After a period in disfavor,
Burns at the moment is highly esteemed for his support of the
President's revised economic policy. But the assistant's point about
ideologues was sound: Moynihan and Burns were believers among
nonbelievers, they fought with each other and for their beliefs, and
the likes of them are no longer to be found at the Nixon White
House. The Texas pyrotechnics of Treasury Secretary John Connally, who functions as an *ex officio* staff assistant, shouldn't be
but often are mistaken for passion. Soon after he joined the Cabinet in February, Connally indicated with a genial grin that he was
prepared to support any side of any argument the President

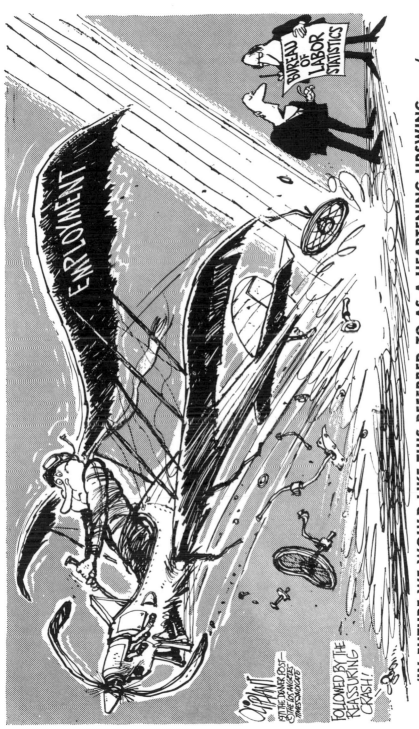

'IN FUTURE WE WOULD LIKE THIS REFERRED TO AS A HEARTENING UPSWING . . .'

wanted him to support. In his capacity as Mr. Nixon's "chief economic spokesman," he has done so with gusto and brilliance.

The practice of pragmatism, Nixon style, exacts a certain toll. Witness the experience and humiliation of Paul McCracken, chairman of the President's Council of Economic Advisers. *The Washington Post* of July 28 published an article, signed by McCracken, that in retrospect amounts to a detailed denunciation of the domestic economic policy Mr. Nixon announced on August 15. On August 16, McCracken applauded the announced policy and he has worked to justify and implement it since then. The derision aimed at McCracken should be aimed at the Nixon establishment. John Kenneth Galbraith had irritated some of that establishment's more sensitive members with a biting critique of pre-August Nixon policy. The Office of Communications Director Herbert Klein was instructed to produce an authoritative rebuttal and get it printed. A Klein assistant first asked George Shultz, the director of the Office of Management and Budget, to write the rebuttal. Shultz passed the buck to McCracken, who finished the piece a couple of days before it appeared in the *Post.* The snapper on this otherwise drab story is that both Shultz and McCracken knew in late July that Mr. Nixon was contemplating the drastic shift in policy he announced on August 15. What they didn't know, and Mr. Nixon didn't know until August 12, was that he was going to announce it so soon. Shultz and McCracken supposed that the turnabout would come, if at all, in late September or early October. They hoped against hope that an economic upsurge in the meantime would validate the previous policy. If not, and the great reversal occurred after all, they figured that the article would be forgotten by the time the President discarded the policy that Shultz and McCracken among others had devised and defended.

Perhaps the most telling testament to the power of Nixon pragmatism is the ease with which the President scuttled his welfare reform program. He said later, much later than such proponents of it as HEW Secretary Elliot Richardson hoped he would, that he hadn't meant to scuttle it. But he had, at least for purposes of passage at the present session of Congress. An interesting thing about the scuttling is the pathetically low price that Mr. Nixon put on the welfare program. A White House "fact sheet" that supplemented the Nixon speech of August 15 gave casual readers the impression that the President proposed to save $1.1 billion in

1972 expenditures by postponing the effective date of his Family Assistance Act from July 1, 1972 to July 1, 1973. George Meany of AFL-CIO said as late as Sunday, September 5, that the President was proposing by this means to "take $1.1 billion from the poor." The fact is that when Mr. Nixon decided to include welfare deferral in his speech he was told by his advisers that it would reduce 1972 expenditures by $150 million; the rest of the $1.1 billion was to come from items identified only as "and other." The Office of Management and Budget strove frantically through the following fortnight to find and put believable dollar numbers on the "and other." George Shultz finally proffered to the House Ways and Means Committee a tabulation that bore very little resemblance to the original "fact sheet" and was loaded with questionable estimates of anticipated expenditure reductions. There is a sort of paper truth, for instance, in the claim that postponement of general revenue sharing will save another $1.1 billion in this fiscal year. But to suggest that the deferral of a program that is given no chance whatever of early enactment will save a penny that hasn't already been "saved" is closer to lying than I'd have expected the Administration to get. Shultz testified on the day the President asked a joint session of Congress to approve his new economic policy. Mr. Nixon said his proposed expenditure cuts came to $4.7 billion, the figure he had used on August 15. Shultz put the total at $5 billion. Ah, well. What's a difference of $300 million, between pragmatists?

September 25, 1971

XXVII

Reform at the FTC–I

One of the wonders of Nixon's Washington is the reform and performance of the Federal Trade Commission since the Republicans took charge of it in January 1970. An agency that had come to exemplify the very worst features of federal regulation—sloth, partisan and personal cronyism, excessive regard for the commercial and industrial predators that it was supposed to police in the public interest—has in less than two years been brought to new life, reorganized and restaffed with young and aggressive regulators, and set upon courses of action and policy that, if allowed to proceed to real fulfilment, could powerfully affect the nation's economic system and change it for the better.

The whole thing defies belief. In the liberal theology, it cannot have happened and it cannot be permitted to go on happening; it is not the kind of behavior to be expected of Richard Nixon or of any Republican President and administration. It is difficult, all but impossible, for the critic to credit Mr. Nixon with either the intention to begin so sweeping a reform or a determination to let it continue to a point, not as yet reached, of genuine and lasting effectiveness. The doubt is not confined to orthodox liberals. The September 10 *Wall Street Journal* printed a report that the FTC's reformist Republican chairman, Miles Kirkpatrick, was about to be offered an appellate judgeship. Another story had it that Kirkpatrick might be appointed ambassador to Belgium. The implication was that the President had a bellyful of FTC reform and of the complaints from businessmen and politicians that naturally resulted. A White House spokesman did little to quiet the rumors with a tepid remark that he had no reason to believe that the President was displeased with Kirkpatrick and his management of FTC. Kirkpatrick himself, disturbed by the uneasiness the reports were causing among his staff, had to dispose of them with an oral statement that he hadn't been offered and didn't expect to be offered any other job and wouldn't accept another job if it were offered. My inquiries at the White House convinced me that the rumors didn't come from the President or from any responsible member of his staff, though some of the political operators around him may have planted the reports in an effort to suggest to Mr. Nixon that he could, if he would, rid himself of an intolerable nuisance by entrusting FTC to a less active reformer and enforcer.

An understanding of the President's attitude toward FTC requires a look back to the Eisenhower years and to the tragedy that overtook Sherman Adams when he was caught at meddling with a commission inquiry into the trade practices of a New England textile manufacturer, Bernard Goldfine. President Eisenhower had to fire Adams, a trusted assistant who until then had an unblemished reputation for integrity and high ability. The episode indelibly identified the FTC to Richard Nixon, then the Vice President, as a potential source of grief and trouble for any President who let it fall into lax ways or let himself and his own staff be tarred with its sins. That memory, plus thorough familiarity with the inherent defects and vulnerabilities of all regulatory agencies in a political system, prepared President-elect Nixon to believe the devastating charges that "Nader's Raiders," seven young lawyers and law students who were loosed upon FTC by Ralph Nader in 1968, published in a report released just before Mr. Nixon took office in 1969. They found that Paul Rand Dixon, the commission's

Democratic chairman since 1961, had turned it into "a patterned and intricate deceptive practice unto itself."

Then came a fascinating display of the Nixon technique. The new President could not bear the thought of appearing to respond directly to the criticisms of so bold and outlandish a maverick as Ralph Nader. Mr. Nixon asked the American Bar Association to conduct a fresh "study and professional appraisal of the FTC." Miles Kirkpatrick, then a distinguished Philadelphia antitrust lawyer and chairman of ABA's antitrust section, headed the commission that made the requested study. Its report, completed in September, sustained in spades the substantive Nader criticisms and refuted the suspicion that Mr. Nixon had prearranged a stacked judgment. The ABA report said that FTC should be abolished if its "several serious and pervasive deficiencies" in leadership, in staff, in policy and performance were not corrected. The first essential for needed change, the study concluded, was the appointment of "an outstanding chairman" who was endowed with "sufficient strength and independence to resist pressures from Congress, the Executive Branch, or the business community that tend to cripple effective performance by the FTC."

Mr. Nixon, amply forewarned, had chosen his "outstanding chairman" when the ABA report appeared. He was Caspar Weinberger, a San Francisco attorney who in 1969 was Governor Ronald Reagan's state finance director. Weinberger later said that the President, during a talk at the Western White House in August about FTC, told him to "go in there and clean it up and you won't have any trouble from me." Cynics doubted that Weinberger would make any trouble for the President or for the businessmen and industrialists who were subject to FTC regulation. He went to work at FTC in January 1970, began a vigorous reorganization and re-staffing of the commission, and was just beginning to apply himself to matters of policy when, after only six months in the chairmanship, he was jerked out of the job and appointed deputy director of the new Office of Management and Budget. Again the doubters had a romp: it was a typical Nixon sham, even the sham was over, and FTC was going to remain its old and discredited self. The romp ended until further notice when the President chose for his second chairman none other than Miles Kirkpatrick, the guiding mentor of the ABA study.

Chairman Kirkpatrick is a Washington oddity, a nominal Republican who has never been discernibly involved in party politics and in his 13 months at FTC has appeared to be immune to the political pressures that must and do bear upon the chairmen and members of all regulatory agencies. There is about him, at age 53, a patrician air of elegance and rectitude. Some of his colleagues and associates perceive in him a quality of naiveté, a sheltering innocence that seems to the earthier types around him to provide him with a kind of inbuilt protection against pressures. A lawyer with his experience—he listed 31 corporate clients in a report to the Senate Commerce Committee—cannot be all that innocent, of course. But the impression exists and it lends an aura of unreality to the reformist bustle over which he presides at FTC.

The beginnings of reform are evident in, among other things, a rigorous process of staff recruitment and enforced retirements. Some 85 recruits, mostly young lawyers and a few economists, have been hired in the past year or so. Robert Pitofsky, a New York University law professor who supervised the ABA study group's staff and drafted the ABA report, heads a reorganized Bureau of Consumer Protection. Alan S. Ward, a former antitrust attorney at the Department of Justice, directs a newly invigorated Bureau of Competition. Lawrence G. Meyer, a former Justice attorney and assistant to Senator Robert Griffin of Michigan, is the chief policy planner. Michael Mann, a Boston College economist, has taken over the recently moribund Bureau of Economics, the source of the commission's basic research. They are young (ages 30 to 42), imbued with a sense of mission, and prepared to believe that Mr. Nixon and their chairman, Kirkpatrick, are prepared to give them their heads and let them make the FTC an effective shaper and regulator of the economy.

It's perverse of me, no doubt, but the figure among this galaxy of zeal and talent who interests me the most is the FTC's executive director, Basil Mezines. He is in his early 40s, a veteran of 20 years with FTC, an unabashed careerist who speaks with engaging frankness of his readiness to serve his master of the moment and of the joy he derives from the power that his masters confer upon him. Mezines is viewed with the deepest possible suspicion by the staff attorneys and economists who hope and imagine that they are serving some higher purpose than their own advancement. Their suspicion is reflected in the 1969 Nader report and in a later Nader study, published last summer, of antitrust policy and enforcement at FTC and Justice. In this adverse and fairly prevalent view, Mezines is the man at FTC through whom the White House staff can and does convey covert directives. Who bullies and chastens staff attorneys for giving the commission's corporate victims a hard time? Mezines, of course. Who at the commission's power levels is ever ready to hear with sympathy the complaints of aggrieved respondents? Again, Mezines.

The Nixon assistants who might, if all this is so, be supposed to be in intimate touch with Mezines are Peter Flanigan, the White House man responsible for liaison with the regulatory agencies, and Fred Malek, the President's chief recruiter and placer of senior appointees. Mezines said the other day that he has never met or talked with Flanigan or Malek or anybody on their staffs. "I'd like to know some of these fellows," he said. "If they want to talk to me, I'd be delighted. If they have higher things in mind for me, I'd sure like to know it. But I never hear from them."

Mezines, who devoted 10 years to the service and cultivation of Chairman Dixon, had been put by Caspar Weinberger at the head of the Bureau of Competition when the new chairman, Kirkpatrick, chose him to be executive director. In that position he is in effect the commission's chief personnel officer, the chairman's right-hand generalist, and a contributor to basic policy. "I wanted the job," he said. "I wanted the power, I wanted to straighten this place out, and I did." The rigor he displayed in straightening it out, partly through convincing entrenched staff veterans that it was time for them to retire without fuss or trouble, seemed to the second Nader study group to deprive the discards of the due process to which they were entitled. Mezines took this and rougher criticism in good spirit, holding with some reason that the Naderites simply couldn't bring themselves to credit him with anything praiseworthy. He was grateful for the first report's acknowledgement that he was a hard worker among a bunch of drones, and he detected a note of rather grudging respect in the second Nader study. "The overall effect," he said, "is that I'm a mean son of a bitch, and I guess that's probably true."

The presence of Basil Mezines (pronounced mehzeenness) at the right hand of the FTC's gentlemanly chairman, Miles Kirkpatrick, somehow makes the FTC phenomenon more believable than it would be without him or somebody like him there. If a Mezines can thrive at the top of the reforming FTC, and have quite a lot to do with the reforms, the institution cannot be completely out of tune with the Nixon administration. Its future in its new guise may be more secure than the cynics, myself included, are as yet inclined to believe it is.

October 2, 1971

———

For a further look at the FTC, see Chapter XXIX.

XXVIII

On the Road

Here are some glimpses and impressions of Mr. Nixon as he showed himself on September 25 and 26, accepting the obeisance of Walter Hickel and meeting the Emperor of Japan in Alaska and, on the way there, playing the part of a busy and happy President and candidate for reelection in 1972 in the states of Montana, Oregon and Washington. He seemed to me to be variously at his inane worst and his gracious best. According to his spokesmen, he seemed to himself to be at his best throughout the expedition. They said that he was "well satisfied" with the whole performance when, after a long flight home on the third day, he and Mrs. Nixon choppered from Andrews Air Force Base to the White House, changed into dinner clothes, and went off to a sumptuous and slightly premature celebration of Mrs. Mamie Eisenhower's 75th birthday.

The first stop at Kalispell, Montana, was said to have been at the urging of Mike Mansfield, the Democratic leader in the Senate, who presumably figured that an appearance with the President would do him and the state's Democratic Party as much good as it would do Mr. Nixon and the Republicans. Kalispell is a small town in the northwest corner of the state, near the Canadian

border and Glacier National Park and also near Libby Dam, a
$482 million project that, when completed, will be part of the US
and Canadian Columbia River power and water-control system.
At Kalispell's airport, for the benefit of some 5000 rural Mon-
tanans, Mr. Nixon briskly saluted the statesmanship and national
importance of Senator Mansfield, the beauty of the surrounding
"Big Sky Country," and his own efforts to achieve "a generation
of peace" with his policy of withdrawal from Vietnam, the imminent honor to Emperor Hirohito, and a forthcoming visit to Communist China. The latter event, he took care to say at Kalispell
and at every subsequent stop, was surely going to occur "at a later
time" despite the current and mystifying signs of disturbance in the
Peking leadership.

At Libby Dam, after a chopper ride over the mountains and
forests of the Glacier area, Mr. Nixon forewent his usual pleasure
in arranging groups for the press photographers and let Senator
Mansfield pose state and local dignitaries with the President. He
walked up to five workers, all of whom were wearing hard hats,
and asked, "Do you wear hard hats?" Back at Kalispell, he indicated that he had noted from his helicopter "the blotches on the
landscape" caused by timber cutting and said with balanced earnest-
ness that "what we need is a balance of course—a balance in
terms of preserving and conserving the environment but at the
same time of allowing the development of course of the lumber industry." He also said that he wanted to see lots of trailer parks
installed in the wilds so that "people of modest means" can "go to
these beautiful places." He recalled with approval the trailers "lined
up by the hundreds" in a state park near his California home at
San Clemente. A reporter asked, "Will that not destroy the scenery
in the area, Mr. President?" Nixon answered: "No. The way
they've set up the trailer parks, if you take San Clemente's example—it's done in a beautiful way. It's set up so that it looks just
like a motel. You have it contoured properly and it's done in the
proper way. And as far as the scenery is concerned, scenery is
great but it isn't any good if people can't use it."

Aloft again and en route to Portland, Oregon, Mr. Nixon announced that he was about to intervene personally, for the first
time in his presidency, in a labor dispute. After a session in his

Portland hotel suite with Harry Bridges, leader of striking long-shoremen who had tied up the West Coast ports, and Ed Flynn, the industry negotiator, the President claimed only that he had imparted to them "a new sense of urgency" and maybe, or maybe not, helped get the bargainers "off dead center." Western media editors and executives had assembled in Portland for a briefing on Nixon policy by Cabinet officers and the President. Instead of boring the audience with prepared remarks, Mr. Nixon invited questions. His most interesting answer indicated that he was content with the present balance of strategic power between the US and the Soviet Union and did not share Defense Secretary Melvin Laird's alarm, expressed of late with increasing emphasis, over the growth of Soviet nuclear missile installations. A questioner quoted Mrs. Nixon's reported remark in Washington, to a group of lady journalists, that the trouble with appointing a woman to one of the two vacancies on the Supreme Court is that "the best qualified women are too old." A traveling reporter in the room said later that Mr. Nixon appeared to be extremely unhappy. He paused, cleared his throat, and said with a feeble laugh that "any politician who says a woman is too old is nuts." He ended a vague elaboration of his search for nominees who share his "general judicial philosophy" with the observation, presumably meant to be funny, that "even an old woman could have that philosophy."

Mr. Nixon made some more trouble for himself when he confided to the editors that he was going to have "a significant announcement" the next day at the Atomic Energy Commission plant and laboratories in Hanford, Washington. A statement handed to reporters during the flight from Portland to Walla Walla and Hanford amounted to nothing more than a pious expression of confidence in the future of the next generation of breeder reactors which are in an early stage of research at Hanford. A second statement, hastily composed aboard the President's plane between Portland and Walla Walla, committed Mr. Nixon to seeking money and authority to build two breeder development plants instead of the one previously contemplated. What the scientists and workers at Hanford wanted to know was whether the first plant is to be established there, instead of somewhere else, in order to arrest the recent decline of employment among them. That depends on AEC decisions yet to be made, and Mr. Nixon's press party left Hanford with a feeling that he'd have been wiser if he'd avoided the place. His only positive assertion at Hanford was that he wasn't intimidated by the unsolved problems of radiation and pollution that are plaguing and delaying the development of nuclear power for industrial and other peaceful uses. "In terms of nuclear power," he said, "we must not be afraid. We must explore it."

Walter Hickel, the former Secretary of the Interior who was fired last year, awaited the President at Anchorage, Alaska. Hickel's book, *Who Owns America?*, had just come out. It is written in a rather smug tone of dislike, close to contempt, for the President. It reflects, to say the least, Wally Hickel's belief that he and not Mr. Nixon understands that the people own America and suggests that this gulf of comprehension led to their bitter parting. By mutual and prior consent, carefully nurtured by Republican Senator Ted Stevens of Alaska during months of negotiation with Nixon associates, all of that was set aside if not forgotten when Wally greeted the President on the lawn of the Hickel home. It was too clear for comfort that Mr. Nixon had been persuaded that Hickel might be useful to him in Alaska and maybe elsewhere during the 1972 presidential campaign. Both men, facing the cameras and exchanging banalities ("Have you ever been in Kalispell?," Nixon said to Hickel), had the grace to seem embarrassed. So did Hickel's successor, Rogers Morton, who promised to throw a party for Wally the next time he was in Washington.

That night a President of the United States and an Emperor of Japan met for the first time, on the first occasion in 2631 years that an Emperor of Japan had left his country. On September 26, 1941, Emperor Hirohito told his military chieftains that he deplored their plans for war and did not order them to abandon the plans. On September 26, 1945, the Emperor motored from his palace to the US Embassy in Tokyo and did homage to the American conqueror, General MacArthur. On this September 26, frail at 70, trembling in the Alaskan chill and at times forgetful of his cues, Hirohito accepted the courtesies of President Nixon and flew on to Europe. Mr. Nixon, a connoisseur and exploiter of historic firsts, behaved with great dignity. Watching him and the little Emperor under the lights, in a vast hangar resounding with the clatter of artillery salutes and trumpets, I was proud of the President. It was a nice though probably meaningless thing for him to do, and he did it well.

October 9, 1971

XXIX

Reform at the
FTC—II

The rules that in principle govern the relationship between the Nixon White House and the Federal Trade Commission, along with other regulatory agencies, are set forth in a memorandum dated May 21, 1969. The memorandum was signed and distributed to the Nixon staff on that date by Peter M. Flanigan, the assistant who oversees White House dealings with the agencies. Flanigan, a wealthy recruit to the Nixon staff from Wall Street, is regarded with considerable suspicion in the White House press room and by some members of Congress who have charged him with serving his own and the financial community's interest at the public expense. None of the charges has ever seemed convincing to me. I take him up to now to be a capable servant of the President, with talents and connections that arise naturally but not harmfully from his background. The memo in which he defines the staff relationship with the agencies is refreshingly free of the cant about the separation of executive and regulatory responsibilities that tends to fog up discussion of the subject. In condensed paraphrase (I am not at liberty to quote it precisely), the substance of it follows:

The primary responsibility of the regulatory agencies is to Congress. They have a duty to investigate, prosecute and judge the cases before them. Any executive interference with this quasi-judicial function would be highly improper. Any expression of interest by the White House staff in the outcome of any pending case or any attempt to influence the outcome would be illegal. It is important that members of the White House staff avoid even the appearance of interest in agency cases or their outcome. However, and in spite of these considerations, sensitive matters often arise which do require official or informal contacts with the commissioners or staffs of these agencies. The policies and findings of these agencies often interact heavily with the policies of the executive branch. There is, therefore, occasion for White House staff contact with these agencies. But members of the staff should keep the Flanigan office informed of any contact and should notify designated members of the Flanigan staff IN ADVANCE of any contact, to make sure that it is appropriate. Members of the White House staff may listen to comments and views on agency cases when they are volunteered by parties to the cases or their representatives. However, such visits or the submission to White House staff members of written briefs should not be encouraged. Better still, they should be sidestepped and avoided whenever possible. Members of the White House staff should not inquire about the status of pending cases. Instead, anyone who asks that such inquiries be made should be told to contact the agency directly.

So far as I have been able to determine, the Flanigan rules have been followed to the letter, and then some, at and with the FTC. The only White House contacts that I have identified at that agency have been with Miles Kirkpatrick, the Philadelphia antitrust lawyer who was appointed to the commission and designated chairman in 1970. According to him, to three of the four other commissioners, to all of FTC's bureau heads, and to several commission attorneys who are breathing volcanoes of suspicion, there has been no interference from the Nixon White House in any matter pending before the commission. In a critical and stupendously thorough study of FTC's antitrust practices by one of Ralph Nader's teams, there is not a single allegation of White House intervention in a pending case. Mark Silbergeld, a former FTC lawyer who joined Nader's research staff in August and is no apologist for the FTC bureaucracy or the Nixon administration, said the other day that he never knew or heard of an instance of White House intervention during six years at the commission, including the first two-and-a-half Nixon years.

An important caveat is made explicit in the Flanigan memorandum and is enlarged upon by Flanigan in conversation. Overall commission policy, as distinct from specific and pending cases, is considered to be a matter of legitimate and necessary interest to the President and to his assistants, principally Flanigan in FTC affairs. Policy influences the outcome of cases, of course, so in this sense the detached innocence of the Nixon White House is far from totally innocent and inclusive. Only one instance of expressed White House policy affecting the outcome of cases has been cited to me, though there probably are others. Flanigan indicated to Chairman Kirkpatrick, in one of their infrequent meetings, that the Administration would like to have the controversial problem of analgesics (pain relievers) and the often exaggerated claims of rival advertisers dealt with through a general commission rule, which would have the force of law, rather than through individual cases against competing companies. This the FTC is in process of doing.

Policy is at the core of several issues that are shaping up for decision. Whether to sustain and carry to its logical conclusion a massive attack upon deceptive advertising practices, including requirements that the perpetrators of false claims acknowledge their lies in later advertisements and perhaps even recompense cheated buyers, is one such issue. Hearings to be opened in late October on the social impact of advertising, particularly TV ads, could draw the FTC into areas and depths of controversy it has never entered before. Herbert Klein, the President's communications director, said recently that the trend endangers press freedom, but it is said at the commission that the White House staff has made no private complaints. A looming issue of immense import is whether the structure of highly concentrated industries, in which a few producers and suppliers dominate their markets, inevitably leads (as the "structuralists" maintain) to inflated prices and other abuses and in itself constitutes a violation of the antitrust laws. If the FTC brings itself to this conclusion, even in a relatively minor case, the result could be the forced breaking up of General Motors, for instance, into four or five competing automobile companies. An FTC attorney who is doing his best to lead the commission in that direction said not long ago that this or any other administration "would dig up this place and pour salt in the hole" if the commissioners let it happen. Yet the commissioners are allowing their staffs to research and emphasize in their case presentations the effects of concentrated industry structures, in a significant departure from the traditional antitrust proposition that the misbehavior of individuals rather than the inherent consequences of industry and market composition destroy competition and violate the law. Peter Flanigan nodded with interest but didn't comment when I mentioned this as an emerging policy issue of presumable concern to the President. Flanigan did say that the initiation of an FTC case involving the structural issue (an effort to force the dissolution of Warner-Lambert's 1968 merger with another big pharmaceutical company, Parke-Davis) was one of several commission actions that hit the White House "like a bolt from the blue." Another stunner, according to Flanigan, was a series of cases in which the commission is questioning the legality of exclusive franchises such as those commonly granted to Coca-Cola and other soft-drink bottlers.

The Nixon people consider that they have three appointees on the present commission. They are Kirkpatrick, who has encouraged the trends just mentioned and others of potentially equal importance; David S. Dennison, a former Republican congressman from Ohio, who has generally supported Kirkpatrick; and Everette MacIntyre, a veteran Democratic holdover. Mary Gardiner Jones, a very nominal Republican, was appointed by President Johnson. Because MacIntyre has passed the legal retirement age, his tenure has to be annually renewed by the President. So far, it has been. The other Democrat, ex-chairman Paul Rand Dixon, is safe in office until 1974. Not the least of the FTC's current oddities is the fact that the two Democrats constitute the commission's conservative minority. It's the Republicans who cause observers to wonder how long Mr. Nixon can and will put up with his reformed FTC.

October 16, 1971

XXX

Out of Phase

Late in the afternoon of Tuesday, October 5, four of Mr. Nixon's advisers forgathered with him at the White House. They were Treasury Secretary John B. Connally; Chairman Paul McCracken of the Council of Economic Advisers; Herbert Stein, a Council member, and George Shultz, director of the Office of Management and Budget. In their capacities as members of the Cabinet-level Cost of Living Council, the body the President had set up to administer his 90-day freeze of wages, prices and rents, they had been working since August 15, when the freeze was announced, to devise the "strong, effective follow-on program" with which Mr. Nixon intended to keep the national economy under control for as long as he deems necessary after the initial freeze ends on November 14. Although his advisers were reluctant to admit the fact, in fear that the elaborate and publicized consultations with labor, management, consumer and other groups that had followed the August 15 announcement would be made to seem an empty farce, the President had in mind at that time and had outlined to his planners the essentials of the system he expected them to recommend. As he indicated publicly on September 16, he wanted it to be concentrated on the control of wages and prices "in major industries"; to operate so far as possible with the voluntary cooperation of labor and management; and, in the predictable event that voluntary cooperation would not always be sufficient, to be administered from the top by an official body, the Cost of Living Council, with full power to require compliance with the standards set and the decisions made in particular cases by the group or groups established to determine the permissible levels of controlled wages and prices. "This is the direction," he said, "that I have given to those working on the programs."

Three principal issues remained to be resolved at the October 5 meeting, two days before the President was to announce the "Phase II" system to become effective on November 15. They were whether he should ask Congress to add the power to control interest and dividends to his present authority (under the Economic Stabilization Act of 1970) to control wages, prices and rents; whether he should also ask Congress to extend the stabilization act for a year beyond next April 30, when it expires, and thus acknowledge that the country is in for a prolonged period of control; and, the question in most serious dispute among his advisers, whether some sort of "numerical standard" that would at least indicate the degree of increase in wages and prices to be permitted should be announced. Whether to seek arbitrary power to control profits had never been the issue among the President's planners that it was in the press. The President had said he was against it, and that was that.

The chief proponent of an announced numerical standard, Chairman Arthur Burns of the Federal Reserve Board, was told that night that the President had bought the idea, though in a highly qualified way. Mr. Nixon himself would not announce a numbered goal or even refer to one in his televised speech. A supplemental "background paper" to be prepared by the Cost of Living Council and issued at the White House in conjunction with the speech would say only that the intended goal was to reduce the annual rate of increase in consumer prices from the present level of around six percent to two or three percent by the end of 1972. George Shultz argued to the very last against doing that much, partly out of conviction and also to make sure that the President

THE PAY BOARD WILL NOW COME TO ORDER

understood the risks involved. To declare a target, Shultz maintained, would diminish the flexibility that he considered essential and would also invite a judgment that the whole effort had failed if the target was not attained. Shultz adamantly opposed any public translation of the vague price target into the actual levels of permissible wage and price increases (six to eight percent) that it implied and to this extent he prevailed over his absent antagonist, Arthur Burns. The other two issues were decided without argument. Congress would be asked to extend the stabilization act into 1973 and, in the new version, authorize the control of interest and dividends if, as the President was to say he didn't think likely, the voluntary holddown on which he relied during the 90-day freeze ceased to work satisfactorily.

The President's speech described the new system in a general way. For the gut of what was intended, the source document was the White House background paper. Herbert Stein completed the draft at 1 A.M. on the day of the speech. It was held in tightest secrecy until midafternoon, when others concerned finished clearing it. The paper was distributed thereafter to journalists at background briefings by "White House officials" through the afternoon and early evening but not—unfortunately, as things developed—to the management and labor spokesmen who were briefed by the same officials, in groups and individually, throughout the day. The paper made it perfectly clear, as Mr. Nixon has been trying not to say of late, that the Cost of Living Council was to have complete powers of review and amendment over the basic decisions of the two bodies, a 15-member Pay Board and a seven-member Price Commission, that were to set overall pay and price standards and decide in particular cases whether wage settlements and price changes did or didn't exceed the permitted levels. The Council was to set initial wage and price standards if, as was all too likely, the Pay Board and Price Commission had not had time to do it by November 14. It also was to designate the "major industries" in which management and unions would have to ask prior permission before increasing wages and prices; the larger number that would be required to report wage and price decisions to the Pay Board and the Price Commission and, through them, to the Cost of Living Council and await approval by those bodies; and that much larger number of businesses and employes that would be subject only to spot checks of their wage and price increases.

The controversial nub was whether the Pay Board and the five labor members to sit on it, with five management and five "public" representatives, would have a completely free hand, as George Meany of AFL-CIO and other labor dignitaries had demanded, or in ultimate effect would be subject to the Cost of Living Council and, through it, to the President. This should never have been in question, but it was. Both the White House paper and Secretary Connally, at a press conference the day following the Nixon speech, said in the plainest possible terms that both the Pay Board and the Price Commission *were* subject in fundamental essentials to Council review and control. Mr. Nixon had said on September 16 that he rejected the notion of a completely autonomous wage board. The White House out, the chosen way around this troublesome fact was that the Pay Board's decisions in particular cases would not be subject to appeal to the Council. In that area and that area alone, the Pay Board was to be self-sufficient. At a group briefing for Meany and other labor leaders on the morning of the President's announcement, and in press briefings, the "White House officials" hammered and hammered at the saving point that the Cost of Living Council would not interfere in specific case decisions. All but one of the briefers ducked the repeated efforts of reporters to get them to admit the plain fact that the Council was to have what amounted to a power of veto over the general decisions of the Pay Board and the Price Commission. At a briefing for TV and radio reporters, Herbert Stein broke the agreed rule of reticence when he was asked whether the Council could "veto the recommended standards." He answered: "They can be vetoed if we consider them inconsistent with the purposes of the program."

That blew it. Apprised of Stein's reply, George Meany declared that he'd been double-crossed and summoned organized labor's moguls to a meeting in Washington to decide whether they would, as they had previously indicated they would, participate in the Pay Board and generally cooperate with the President. Shultz and Secretary of Labor James Hodgson tried to placate Meany with the same old word game. Failing, they got Mr. Nixon to scrawl "Okay, RN" on a revised summary of the role of the Council that said "it will not approve, revise, veto, or revoke *specific* [my emphasis] standards or criteria developed by the Pay Board and

Price Commission." I was told at the White House, shortly before Meany announced that he and his labor friends had got their way and would cooperate, that the new language didn't really change anything. If it didn't, there will be hell to pay.

October 23, 1971

—————

It didn't, and there was.

XXXI

The Rev. Billy's Day

Along the route that Mr. Nixon and his companion in a White House limousine, the Reverend Billy Graham, took from the Charlotte, NC, airport to the Charlotte Coliseum, where Billy Graham Day was celebrated on October 15, there were several street-side signs that read as follows: "With the third highest crime rate in the nation, all we need is Liquor by the Drink to put us on top." It may be doubted that the President, busy waving at the crowds and suppressing his normal desire to get out of the car and shake hands, noticed the signs. If he had noticed them, he probably would not have grasped the rather sour joke on him and his friend Billy that a lot of people in Charlotte thought the signs represented. It appeared to these people, presumably including many of the 13,000 who packed the circular hall of the Coliseum, that the President and the Reverend Billy had been trapped into public association with the advocates of legalizing the bar sale of hard liquor in Charlotte and Mecklenburg County. A local judge was to decide the following week whether the citizens of Charlotte and the surrounding county could vote on November 5, as the state legislature had said they could, for and against legalizing sale "by the drink." It was a hot issue in the city and county, the last battle between prohibitionists and the modernists, led by the Charlotte Chamber of Commerce, who argued that the present restriction to package sales made it unduly difficult to attract conventions and otherwise denied the city and its environs full participation in the joys and amenities of the 20th century.

Dragging the liquor issue into the accounts of Billy Graham Day was discouraged in Charlotte. The inventor and principal sponsor of the occasion, President Charles Crutchfield of the Chamber of Commerce, attributed the covert suspicion that it was a factor to the machinations of the prohibitionists. Their leader, Charlotte attorney Allen A. Bailey, declined to discuss the matter for the record. But it was clear that he and his allies, who included many of Charlotte's Protestant pastors, believed and put it about that Mr. Nixon had been gulled. They also felt that the Reverend Billy had acted with something less than the righteous consistency to be expected of a Baptist preacher who was at once Charlotte's most famous native son and, as the President said in his speech, "the evangelist who has been heard by more people in more parts of the world than any in the history of the world." It was said that Billy Graham had been invited to endorse the opposition to bar sales and, from his mountain home across the state at Montreat, had sent word that it was a local issue in which he saw no need to involve himself.

The Chamber of Commerce president, Mr. Crutchfield, is also the president of the Jefferson Standard Broadcasting Company, which operates television and radio stations in Charlotte and elsewhere. He is on a list of some 40 businessmen and communicators who get privileged treatment at the Nixon White House. They are invited from time to time to meet the President at unannounced sessions and to get from him and senior members of his staff briefings on major items of Nixon policy. Among such figures as the chairmen and presidents of General Electric, Westinghouse, Honeywell, US Steel and Atlantic Richfield, and distinguished academics like Milton Friedman of the University of Chicago and Howard Johnson of MIT, Mr. Crutchfield considers himself to be a little fellow. But he's there, he chats with the President, and at a briefing last June 22 he mentioned his plans to arrange a day in Charlotte in honor of his and Mr. Nixon's dear friend, Billy Graham. Mr. Nixon said he'd like to attend. At another briefing in late July, preceded by dinner with Mr. Nixon in the State Dining Room at the White House and climaxed with a private account from Henry Kissinger of his first trip to Peking, the President firmed up his acceptance of the invitation and instructed his staff to fix a date with Crutchfield that would be convenient for the Reverend Billy. Perhaps mindful of his recent refusal to join the fight against bar sales in Charlotte, Graham demurred at first but came around and agreed on October 15. One gathers that he relied upon his old friend from his Charlotte days, Charlie Crutchfield, to knock off any speculation to the effect that the whole thing was a ploy on behalf of loosening the local liquor law by demonstrating in the most public way that the friends of bar sales were also the friends of President Nixon and Billy Graham. Confronted with that speculation, Crutchfield said in private that he thought up Billy Graham Day and had mentioned it to Mr. Nixon before anybody knew that the legislature would allow a referendum on the liquor question this year. Crutchfield prepared a formal statement that said as much, adding that gossip to the contrary "demeaned Dr. Graham," but never issued it.

The upshot was a thoroughly pleasant and invigorating day for all concerned, excepting the aggrieved opponents of bar sales. Billy Graham said that Mr. Nixon is a warm and likeable human being, a tough and courageous President who disdains expediency and compromise. In proof of the latter assertion, Graham raised his magnificent voice to its full organ tone and said: "I remember once I made a suggestion to him. He looked me in the eye and said, *'Billy, that wouldn't be moral.'* " The Reverend Billy then said something that may tell a good deal about how he and Mr. Nixon regard each other. "At that moment," Graham said, "he was the preacher and I was the sinner." Mr. Nixon gazed straight ahead, without a visible quiver. The honoree evoked his boyhood on a dairy farm that is now a forest of stores and office buildings, with the house where he was born tucked in a surviving nook, and recalled that in those days his kind of folks killed their own rats and didn't ask the federal government to do it. The remark drew a nod from Mr. Nixon and tremendous applause from the audience. I found myself connecting it, no doubt unfairly, with the smattering of long-haired youths who displayed antiwar signs and yelled derisively at the President and Reverend Billy on their way to and from the Coliseum. Nixon and Graham actually treated the few dissidents with a show of amused tolerance, at one point raising their fingers in the V-sign of peace and saluting a young man who was screaming "Murderer!"

During the 27 minutes that Mr. Nixon required for his speech, he seemed to be reaching for a way to say the right things about the Reverend Billy without offending the many people who variously are not Protestants, not fundamentalists, and not as responsive as the President is to the Graham gospel. In the course of getting to what the nation owes Billy Graham, the President rendered a fairly complete recital of what the nation owes Richard Nixon. His forthcoming trips to China and Moscow, his efforts to wind down the Vietnam war, his progress toward a generation of peace, and his endeavors to keep America from growing soft while it grows richer and richer, were favorably mentioned. What the nation owes the Reverend Billy, the President finally got around to saying, is the impact of his effort "to inspire in individuals that religious faith which means moral strength and character"—the quality, Mr. Nixon said, that a nation has to have and keep in order to be great and the quality, too, that makes Billy Graham "one of the greatest leaders of our time."

Back at the airport, the President told group after group of farewell handshakers that he'd enjoyed the day enormously. When he asked the Reverend Billy what he thought of the day, Graham said that he accepted the honor for himself and gave the credit to the Lord. Mr. Nixon beamed his approval and, with Secretary of the Treasury John Connally and several other politicos in tow, vanished into the airplane that used to be Air Force One and is now the Spirit of '76.

October 30, 1971

———

Charlotte newspapers and citizens complained afterward that the Secret Service and local authorities roughed up beardies and any others who looked as if they might be inclined to give Mr. Nixon and the Reverend Billy a show of more dissent than was apparent to the President's press party.

XXXII

Two Are Chosen

With some necessary background from the public record, here is the gist of what I hear at the White House and elsewhere about the strange events and behavior that preceded the President's nominations of Lewis F. Powell Jr. and William Rehnquist to be Associate Justices of the Supreme Court.

The story around Washington that the President said "Fuck the ABA!" in a moment of extreme irritation with the American Bar Association and its judiciary committee of 12 eminent lawyers is correct. A printed report that the remark surprised and shocked the White House assistants who heard it is not correct. Mr. Nixon often talks like that; the operative word is one of his favorites. The interesting thing about the use of it in this instance is that Attorney General John Mitchell brought on the situation that vexed the President. In 1969, when he nominated Chief Justice Warren E. Burger, the President excluded his choices for the

Supreme Court from the preliminary ABA review to which prospective nominees for the lower federal courts are customarily subjected. In July of 1970, after the Senate had rejected the nominations of Clement Haynsworth and Harrold Carswell, the Attorney General agreed with Bernard Segal of Philadelphia, then the ABA's president, and Lawrence E. Walsh of New York, then and now chairman of the ABA judiciary committee, that ABA review of Supreme Court prospects might save the President from the kind of embarrassing and belated disclosures that did in Haynsworth and Carswell. Mr. Nixon must have assented to the change. Officially, however, it was John Mitchell's doing. His agreement with the ABA, formalized by letter, obligated him to submit the names of possible nominees to the Walsh committee for its review before he recommended them to the President. But, as nobody except the President seems to have realized at the time, it did not obligate Mr. Nixon to consider for nomination only prospects that the Attorney General had cleared with the committee and recommended to the President. It was a tricky arrangement, loaded with potential trouble, and the trouble inherent in it burst upon all concerned after the late Justice Hugo Black and Justice John M. Harlan retired from the Court.

Mitchell stipulated two conditions in letters to Segal and Walsh. They were that the ABA committee should confine its review and findings to "the professional qualifications" of prospective nominees and should do its utmost to keep the names submitted to it and its checks upon the individuals secret. Accepting both conditions, Walsh said in a reply to Mitchell that "the committee of course will do its best to keep confidential the names you submit." The inference, thoroughly understood by Mitchell, was that the committee's "best" almost certainly would not be enough to prevent discovery and publication of the names, once the committee members began checking with other lawyers all over the country. Walsh also promised Mitchell that the committee would report immediately to him, before its inquiries were completed, any early indications that a prospective nominee was likely to be found unqualified. Both of these factors, the understood probability of premature publication and early warning of adverse findings, figured in the fantastic smozzle that clouded the nominations that Mr. Nixon finally made.

The President's personal view of the nomination process also

POWELL & REHNQUIST

I AM THE PRESIDENT

I HAD MY MONEY ON J.EDGAR.

figured in the murky drama. It is a view that was conditioned in part by his experience with the Haynsworth and Carswell nominations. He is said to remain as convinced as he was in 1969 that the Attorney General served him well when he recommended Judge Haynsworth for promotion to the Supreme Court from the Fourth Circuit Court of Appeals. The fatal flaws in the Attorney General's preliminary checks on Haynsworth, having mostly to do with the nominee's stock holdings and financial connections with a few litigants, are blamed by the President upon the natural hazards of investigation, not upon Mitchell. There is said to be a difference, though not a very critical difference, in the President's evaluation of the Carswell debacle. The Attorney General's acknowledged failure to discover, in time to prevent a disastrous nomination, the indications of sheer racist prejudice in Carswell's past and remnants of it in his performance as a federal judge in Florida was too glaring to be overlooked. But even that failure served chiefly, in the President's mind, to strengthen and confirm his distrust of the processes of investigation upon which he must rely when he is choosing among lawyers and judges who are known to him only by reputation and through the recommendations of others. Mr. Nixon's ideal nominee for the Supreme Court is one whom he knows well enough to judge for himself, and the only nominee to date who has fully met that requirement is Chief Justice Burger. "I have known him for 21 years," the President said when he nominated Burger, and he has not been wholly happy and comfortable with any nominee since then.

It was in this general state of mind, I am told at the White House, that the President let his Attorney General compile a list of six prospective nominees for the two vacancies left by Justices Black and Harlan and submit them for an ABA review to which Mr. Nixon never did attach much value. His initial choice for Justice Black's seat, Congressman Richard H. Poff of Virginia, had become known within days after Poff's name was submitted to the Walsh committee. Poff withdrew when it began to seem that he might get less than a favorable ABA judgment and would, in consequence, have rough going at a Senate confirmation hearing. It was then that reporters began to hear around the White House the opinion that the ABA role was a nuisance, a makeweight, an unnecessary and regretted complication in a process that was perilous and complex enough at best.

Yet the six names went forward. Four people on the list—
Senator Robert Byrd of West Virginia; Judge Charles Clark of
Mississippi and the Fifth Circuit Court of Appeals; Judge Paul H.
Roney of Florida and the same court; and Judge Sylvia Bacon of
the District of Columbia Superior Court, the city of Washington's
lowest trial court—are acknowledged now to have been so much
window-dressing, Byrd, the assistant Democratic leader in the
Senate, was more than that for a few days, but he was dropped
when it developed that he had never practiced law or taken a bar
examination. The seriously considered candidates on the list were
Herschel Friday of Little Rock, a locally distinguished attorney
who was recommended and strongly urged upon the President by
the Attorney General, and Judge Mildred Lillie of Los Angeles,
who sits on the state district appellate court for Southern California.

Mitchell submitted the names to the ABA committee chairman,
Lawrence Walsh, late on Tuesday, October 12. Nina Totenberg,
a reporter for the weekly *National Observer,* had the entire list
and moved it on the Dow-Jones financial news wire Wednesday
afternoon. The uproar that followed was ludicrous but damaging.
The President's spokesmen at the White House and Mitchell's at
Justice swore that nobody in either place leaked the list to Miss
Totenberg. She said, days later, that her information didn't come
from the ABA. I noted with interest that senior officials at the
White House and at Justice made no effort whatever to find out
where the leak came from and their spokesmen were obviously
pleased when nobody else found out. I noted with equal interest
that the President and the very few White House assistants who
were concerned with and consulted about the nominations were
not at all surprised when the news leaked that the ABA committee
had voted 11 to 1 that Judge Lillie was not qualified for the
Supreme Court. The committee split, 6 to 6, in finding variously
that Herschel Friday was not qualified and barely qualified.
Lawrence Walsh had kept his promise to warn Mitchell in advance
of any adverse findings.

Two days before the President announced his nominations, he
asked Lewis Powell in Richmond to accept one of them and had
William Rehnquist alerted to the possibility that he might get
the other one. At the same time, he was complaining in the
privacy of his office that the six prospects reviewed by the ABA

were being "pilloried." So they were. But who pilloried them?
And what did Mr. Nixon think he got out of the messy performance?

November 6, 1971

———

Sirs:

I noted John Osborne's piece in *The New Republic* of November
6—particularly his reference to a profane remark attributed to
the President. The President's use of this obscenity in describ-
ing the ABA was supposed to have taken place during a meeting
in the President's office on the morning of Friday, October 2.

I happened to be present for that entire meeting. I would like
to set the record straight: The President did not use the quoted
obscenity at any time during that meeting.

I have great respect for your reporter, John Osborne. He is
one of the ablest observers of the Washington scene and one who
attempts to be as honest as a reporter can be in this city. Un-
happily, his source misinformed him in this instance. The simple
fact is that in the many hours I have spent with the President
I have never heard him use the word attributed to him in Mr.
Osborne's piece.

> *John D. Ehrlichman*
> *Assistant to the President*
> *for Domestic Affairs*

When *The New Republic*'s editors received the foregoing letter,
I asked them to print it without comment and they did. However,
I am constrained to relate a story told me by a reporter who covered Nixon's 1962 campaign for the governorship of California.
Walking away with Nixon from a rural rally that had been poorly
organized and attended, the reporter commiserated with the candidate. Nixon replied, "Oh well, that's what you have to expect from
these fucking local yokels."

In writing my report on the nominations, I left to *New Republic* editors the tasks of identifying and evaluating Powell (a distinguished Richmond attorney) and Rehnquist (an Assistant Attorney General from Arizona). Both of them seemed to me to be qualified nominees. I thought and still think that liberal critics of Rehnquist's conservatism made asses of themselves.

XXXIII

Leadership and Aid

The defeat of the foreign aid bill in the Senate in early November hit the Nixon White House with particular force because it came at a time when things seemed to be going well for the President on the foreign policy front. Mr. Nixon was confident that his imminent report on past and intended withdrawal from Vietnam would further disarm the critics of his war policy and demonstrate a will for peace on his part that they could not convincingly question. Attempts to restrict his freedom of maneuver in Southeast Asia had been repeatedly beaten down in the Senate and the House of Representatives. In the aftermath of Henry Kissinger's second visit to Peking, the President's trip in early 1972 to Communist China was shaping up as a venture with a promise of considerably more substantive accomplishment than had seemed likely when Kissinger returned from his first preparatory journey in July. The announcement that a summit conference in Moscow would follow the Peking visit appeared to place Mr. Nixon in the rewarding posture of a President in full command of his foreign problems, directing a series of historic turns in national attitudes and policy that could, if all went as planned, make him an unbeatable candidate for reelection in 1972.

Beyond the sheer shock of the Senate vote, two factors contributed to the White House malaise. One of them was that the President and the assistants who are supposed to protect him from discomfiting surprise were totally surprised. Former Congressman Clark MacGregor of Minnesota, the President's chief lobbyist, left town on the afternoon of the disaster to make a speech and visit his daughters in New England. Secretary of State Rogers and his departmental lobbyists were equally astounded. The fact that some of the senators who voted down the bill didn't realize that they were killing it instead of merely, as in years past, venting their discontents in a harmless way, did not mitigate the impression that the gap of communication and understanding between the President and Congress was dangerously wide. The second factor was even more painful. The defeat and the White House reaction to it highlighted past and recent flaws of judgment and leadership that marred the nurtured image of a wise and far-sighted President.

The notion, pumped up and magnified by hostile members of the White House press corps, that Mr. Nixon brought the defeat upon himself was absurd. The countervailing pretense that he had nothing to do with it was also absurd. His contributions to public and congressional frustration with foreign aid date back to his 1968 campaign. His line then was "Let us help our friends who help themselves, but let us not help any who help our enemies." The roars of crowd approval that his words and his manner aroused should have indicated to any sensitive observer that Nixon the candidate was playing the game with foreign aid that he played with welfare, professing to support it while appealing to popular dislike of it. Only last April, proposing reforms that many Senate critics of the present programs advocate in principle but have done woefully little to bring about, the President argued that drastic changes are necessary if the country is to have "an effective US foreign assistance program." On a lower plane, his cavalier call in August for a 10 percent cut in foreign aid as part of the budget reductions proposed in connection with his revised economic policy, was more damaging and thoughtless than it was generally perceived to be. Mr. Nixon neither knew nor

'OH, WELL, OFF INTO THE WORLD AGAIN . . .'

seemingly cared where the cut was to come from when he ordered it, and the congenital foes in Congress were justified in taking his action as a signal that foreign aid stood almost as low in the President's priorities as it did in theirs. His crass reaction on October 27 to the display of pleasure at the UN General Assembly after the Taiwan Nationalists were expelled was a witless and unintended, and therefore all the more deplorable, invitation to take out the irritation that he shared with many others in a savage and undiscriminating blow at foreign assistance. It remains true, of course, that the bill was not defeated at the White House. It was defeated in the Senate, in one of that body's least glorious moments. But it may fairly be hoped that Mr. Nixon and his counsellors reflect upon his contributions to the defeat and discern in them, with due humility and a will to correction, the flaws in his judgment and leadership that they illuminate.

This said, any reasonable person must agree with Secretary Rogers's plaintive remark at the White House on November 2 that this of all times was the poorest of times for so gross a blow at a major and necessary instrument of foreign policy. He cited among other reasons the emerging readjustment of the American position in Asia and, by implication, the preparations for the President's approaching personal negotiations with the leaders of Communist China. A degree of secrecy that is remarkable even for the secretive Nixon administration shrouds the preparations. Secretary Rogers discusses what he knows about them with only three officials at State (Under Secretary Alexis Johnson, Assistant Secretary Marshall Green, and Communist affairs specialist Alfred Jenkins), and they are forbidden to discuss the subject either with reporters or with the press officers who normally give journalists the illusion that they are being adequately informed. The White House and State assistants who accompanied Kissinger on his second trip to Peking were forbidden after they returned to say they did or didn't have a good time, much less divulge any fact of substance, however trivial. In one of his very few reportable sessions with the press, Kissinger said little more than that Mr. Nixon will go to Peking after January 1 and that the precise date of the visit will be announced before December 1.

The official guidance from Kissinger at the aforementioned

press conference that no issues "that primarily affect third countries" will be discussed in Peking is somewhat misleading. Every conceivable issue that is worthy of discussion between Mr. Nixon and Premier Chou En-lai and Mao Tse-tung is bound to be of great if not "primary" interest to many "third countries." One such issue is the Nixon approach to a negotiated settlement of the Vietnam war, and it is on the agenda prepared by Kissinger and Chou. This does not affect or alter Kissinger's statement that "we do not expect to settle" the Vietnam war in Peking, meaning that any settlement must be negotiated with Hanoi in Paris and that Mr. Nixon neither expects nor intends to ask the Chinese leaders to further a negotiated settlement. But that does not debar the President from expounding his view of a feasible settlement and inviting Chou En-lai and Mao to expound theirs to him. Nor does it debar a hope that such an exchange of views will promote, at least indirectly, a negotiated settlement that the US and Communist China can live with. After Kissinger's first trip to Peking, the hope and expectation were that Hanoi would have been brought into serious negotiation in Paris before the President goes to Peking. That is still the hope. It was one of the reasons for announcing originally that the Nixon trip could occur as late as next May 1. Whether useful negotiation is still expected before Mr. Nixon goes to Peking, I do not know.

Similar considerations apply to the delicate question of relationships with the Nationalist "Republic of China" on Taiwan. The President does not propose to tell Chou and Mao what they should do about Taiwan, or agree in Peking to anything that the Taiwan government has no choice but to accept. Now that Communist China has been admitted to the UN and Taiwan has been expelled, however, the President is free to an extent that he would not otherwise have been to discuss in Peking the hope that he broadly indicated in his statement of foreign policy last January. The President's hope is that time and experience will close the rift between the two Chinese governments in a way that leaves the Taiwan nationalists substantial autonomy and satisfies the claim of the People's Republic to be the one and only sovereign Chinese power.

November 13, 1971

———

Announcing his next increment of troop withdrawals from Vietnam (nine days after the foregoing was written), Mr. Nixon confirmed my impression that he did indeed expect to discuss Vietnam issues in Peking, and in Moscow as well. I had not the slightest hint that Henry Kissinger had been secretly conducting what he thought "useful negotiation" with Hanoi officials since August 1969—as he and the President disclosed in January 1972.

XXXIV

The Dan Schorr Affair

One of the reasons, perhaps the main reason, why the President invited reporters to question him on November 12, after he announced his intention to withdraw 45,000 more troops from Vietnam, was his hope that he would be asked about Daniel Schorr. Dan Schorr is a CBS correspondent in Washington who was investigated by the FBI last August, ostensibly because he was being considered for appointment to a high government job. Schorr was never told that he was being considered for a job and the job was never identified. The question raised by the belated disclosure of the investigation was whether Schorr really had been considered for a job or whether the whole thing was an exercise in intimidation and retaliation for news reports and interpretations that had frequently annoyed the President and some of his assistants.

Principally because the reporters were in a hurry to break away and file the Vietnam news, the President was not asked about the Schorr affair. After Mr. Nixon, visibly disconcerted by the abrupt termination of the press conference, retired to his Oval Office,

Press Secretary Ronald Ziegler scurried busily around, telling reporters what the President would have said if they had not disappointed him. The import of what Ziegler said the President would have said was that the White House assistants who authorized the FBI investigation had indeed been as stupid as they had to have been if their motives were as pure as Mr. Nixon wanted the press and public to believe they were. Ziegler said the President would have said that the Schorr affair "was handled in a clumsy way." He also said the President recognized merit in the view that people who are being considered for government appointments should be told that they are before the FBI is set upon them. "Therefore," Ziegler concluded in the pious tone that generally marks oblique confessions of past error at the Nixon White House, "the President has ordered that whenever anyone is considered for a government job he always be informed beforehand why a customary FBI check is being made and, if he or she is not interested, then the matter will be dropped right there."

Before the Schorr affair and the circumstances that impelled Mr. Nixon to involve himself in it are further explained, a few relevant facts about the setup at the White House should be noted. The only assistants who have been officially identified with one or another aspect of the Schorr matter are Charles Colson, the President's Special Counsel, and Frederick V. Malek, the chief talent hunter. Colson, a former Boston lawyer, is charged with doing Mr. Nixon's dirtiest dirty work and is extremely good at shielding both himself and the President from provable blame for doing it. He has arranged smears of Democratic candidates for the Senate and has planted news stories designed to shame and discipline persons who have displeased the President (including, for a recent and notable example, Chairman Arthur Burns of the Federal Reserve Board). Colson has also moved in on Communications Director Herbert Klein, covertly taking over most of the operational responsibility for the President's domestic propaganda. Malek is a cold-eyed, coldly loyal young businessman who commands the services of half a dozen junior assistants and keeps tabs on present and prospective vacancies in the upper bureaucracy, partly for the purpose of easing out unsatisfactory incumbents and replacing them with dependable successors. He and the President usually communicate with each other through H. R. Haldeman, the White House chief of staff and the one assistant whose standing with Mr. Nixon moves in only one direction—up. Colson enjoys direct access to the President, but he also reports and is responsible to Haldeman. Neither Malek nor Colson would ever do anything that they don't think the President wants them to do. They would never do anything of importance that they don't *know* Haldeman wants them to do. This fact brings us back to Daniel Schorr. Fooling around in any fashion whatever with so prominent and potent a national journalist and, through him, with the CBS television and radio networks, was bound to have been rated a matter of high importance at the White House. If Bob Haldeman and the President himself swore on a stack of Bibles that Haldeman knew nothing about and had nothing to do with the FBI investigation of Schorr, I wouldn't believe them.

In order to believe that the Nixon administration really did want to hire Schorr, you have to believe that the following sequence of previous events didn't matter or that, if it did, it enhanced the calculated value of getting Schorr off the air and associating him with the Nixon regime. Last March 9, Schorr reported on the Cronkite evening news show that Mr. Nixon had come to wish "that he, the President, had had more time before being rushed into a decision" to recommend and fight for the Safeguard anti-ballistic missile system. Schorr implied in his first report and said flatly on the next night's show that he had been told this by James Fletcher, director-designate of the National Aeronautics and Space Administration, who was said by Walter Cronkite to "have heard the President express some doubts about the [ABM] program." The report enraged Mr. Nixon. Not content with having Ronald Ziegler call a special press briefing and deny that the President and Fletcher had ever discussed the ABM, the President told a gaggle of female reporters that Dan Schorr had "made a statement with regard to the ABM that was totally without foundation and fact." Mr. Nixon added, "You can't allow a little lie." Then, in a classic Nixon weasel, the President said, "Incidentally, when I call it a lie, that is unfair. Because, after all, the man just probably had the wrong information. I am always charitable to my friends." Fletcher told another CBS reporter that "I did not discuss the ABM with the President, ever." He told me the same thing, convincing me—though Schorr to this day sticks to his story—that the report was a mistake perpetrated in the best of faith.

Schorr continued to irritate Nixon people with the kind of reporting that caused James Reston of *The New York Times* to call him "a tough-minded and admirably nosy old pro." His work compounded the soured and exaggerated White House view that CBS's Washington news staff is overloaded with sharp characters who have a tendency to shoot from the hip and to reflect their own prejudices in their news reports, not to mention avowed commentaries. In the story that broke the news of the Schorr investigation, Ken W. Clawson of *The Washington Post* reported that Frank Stanton, the CBS vice chairman, asked for and was granted an audience with Charles Colson last July 15. "Promising only fairness," Clawson wrote, "Stanton invited Colson to talk to him personally when he felt that CBS had failed in its reporting." Colson and Stanton failed to return my telephone calls when I tried to check out these and other references to them in the Clawson story. Ronald Ziegler said the references, including statements that Colson had subsequently complained to Stanton about Schorr, were correct. If I were a CBS reporter, I'd feel more intimidated by such an arrangement that I would by anything, an FBI investigation included, that anybody at the White House could do or arrange to have done to me.

Press Secretary Ziegler, confronted with the storm of cynicism and indignation that followed the *Post* disclosure, said variously that Schorr actually had been "considered for consideration" for a specific job and for several jobs "in the environmental area." He said again and again, in differing words, that "I would simply say that in order for there to be intimidation, the intent has to be there and there is no intention on the part of this administration to proceed in that manner." He repeatedly refused to identify the job or jobs intended for Schorr because to do so would embarrass the incumbents, and then promised to identify *the* job when it is filled by somebody else. Aware that nothing that Ziegler or the President himself could do or say would repair the credibility damage unless a specific job for Schorr was identified, a White House official finally did name one to me—a job that only a fool would have expected Dan Schorr to consider taking. By both Ziegler's and Fred Malek's accounts, the procedures for authorizing FBI investigations of prospective appointees are disgracefully loose. The trouble is, the accounts are deceptive. The procedure is and has been very tight, so tight that only an assistant acting with the President's authority can order an FBI investigation that goes beyond a superficial "name check" to determine whether there is anything against a prospect in existing FBI and Internal Revenue files. The investigation of Schorr was a brief but thorough field check with relatives, neighbors, superiors, other journalists.

CBS was late and cautious in reporting the affair. In a Sunday radio commentary, Schorr eventually said: "I do not know for sure that there was never a government job in mind for me. It seemed, on the face of it, improbable in the light of previous administration reactions toward my reporting. Yet, in a vast bureaucracy, it is possible that someone conceived the idea of trying to hire me, and that some of the processing started."

My guess is that Fred Malek is correct when he says that "somebody for whom I have great respect" recommended Schorr for a job. My further guess is that somebody else killed the idea, but not in time to save the President from having to convict his assistants of believable stupidity.

November 27, 1971

Nixon assistants said in early 1972 that Schorr had been considered for a job with the Council on Environmental Quality. It was not the job named to me in November.

XXXV

Notes from the Cavern

Here are some notes on recent events and trends at the Nixon White House that are not of great significance in themselves but do throw a little light into that shadowy cavern.

The President had a farewell talk the other day with John Price, the last of the bright young men who came to the White House in 1969 with Daniel Patrick Moynihan and, with him, worked up most of the creative ideas that sparked the Administration's first two years. Price, aged 32, a lawyer who doesn't care to practice law, is leaving the Nixon staff to join a New York investment firm and, if the signs continue to seem propitious, to seek the Republican nomination for Congress in a Long Island district. Mr. Nixon wished him well in his congressional venture but, as is the President's custom, avoided an outright endorsement that in any case probably wouldn't do Price much good in a district now represented by Democratic Congressman Lester L.

Wolff. Price is not being replaced on the Domestic Council staff headed by John D. Ehrlichman, the Assistant for Domestic Affairs. Its 26 deputy, special and staff assistants include no less than six "assistant directors." Presumably necessary endeavors occupy all of them, but Ehrlichman does not encourage the kind of personal notice and credit that made Moynihan's shop an especially rewarding place to work in during his time. Price's final chore was a report upon present and possible national urban policy that was required by Congress and will be submitted to it in February. With the departure of Price, only one member and former leader of the Ripon Society, an organization of mildly dissident Republicans, is left in the President's immediate service. The sole survivor of that breed on the staff is Lee Huebner, a speech writer.

Stephen Hess, Moynihan's deputy and chief assistant during the first two years, left the staff in late 1970, shortly before Moynihan returned to the Harvard faculty. Hess has just completed his work as national chairman of the White House Conference on Children and Youth (actually two separate conferences) and at the moment is putting in two months as a *per diem* consultant, doing a survey of cultural organizations based in Washington. His friends understand that he'd like to stay in government, but there doesn't seem to be much chance that he will despite Moynihan's strong endorsement and the friendly interest of Ehrlichman and Leonard Garment, the Nixon assistant who comes closer than any other to filling Moynihan's old role. Ehrlichman and Garment almost succeeded in getting Hess nominated to be director of the federally financed Endowment for the Humanities, an office that disburses some $30 million a year to scholars and groups involved in humanist studies. The news that Hess, a student of politics and co-author of a political biography of Nixon, was in line for the job brought the academic community up in arms. Ehrlichman decided that Mr. Nixon should not be committed to battle in behalf of Hess, despite his acknowledged talents and his past services to the President. Typical of the Nixon procedure in such matters, the choice of whether to stand by Hess or to find a nominee who would be acceptable to the hungry academics was never put up to the President. Ehrlichman made the choice for him. Professor Ronald S. Berman of the University of California, San Diego, a respected scholar and author with comfortably conservative leanings, was nominated by the President in early November.

Another departing assistant is K. Wayne Smith, the chief of
the eight (soon to be 11) systems analysts on Henry Kissinger's
National Security Council staff. There's a certain humor in the
fact that Smith, his predecessor and his successor, Deputy Assistant Secretary of Defense Philip A. Odeen, are distinguished examples of the "whiz kids" whom Mr. Nixon promised to "root
out" of the security establishment in one of his 1968 campaign
speeches. Smith and Alain Einthoven, the arch whiz kid of the
Kennedy-Johnson era at the Pentagon, co-authored a book (*How
Much Is Enough?*) on the nature and importance of systems
analysis, which may be crudely said to be the art of identifying
all the factors of a policy problem and testing proposed solutions
against those factors. One of Smith's NSC analysts, John Andrew
Hamilton Jr., quit in August.

The impression among some of their remaining colleagues at
NSC is that the approach of an election year was one of their
secondary reasons for quitting. A fairly common apprehension
on Kissinger's staff, based in part upon the past experience of
some of its members, is that its chief function in 1972 will be to
bolster the defense and justification of established policies rather
than subject those policies to a continuing process of objective
review. This is not an inspiring prospect for specialists who have
trained themselves to be chronic skeptics. With all respect to
Henry Kissinger, and his assistants do hold him in the highest
respect, his readiness to explain and justify the President's policies
at off-record sessions with all sorts of influential groups tends to
strengthen the assumption that the premium in 1972 will be
upon helping to prove that he and the President have been right
in their foreign policy decisions. Wayne Smith's known reasons
for leaving are less provocative, but they convey some idea of what
it means to work for Kissinger. Apart from the offer of a remu-
nerative private job, Smith concluded that 16 months of 12-hour
days under the Kissinger lash were all that he could take for
a while. Smith's successor, Philip Odeen, presumably knows what
he's getting into. One of his main jobs at the Pentagon has been
to supervise the staff work that precedes the Defense Department's
submissions of budget data and justifications to the NSC Defense
Review Group, which Kissinger heads.

A favored diversion among the President's domestic assistants
is gossip about the present status and probable future of Vice

President Agnew. The most interesting impression relayed to outsiders is to the effect that Agnew is as much in the dark as all of the outsiders and most if not all of Mr. Nixon's assistants are. If the President and the Vice President have discussed the matter, it's the best kept secret at the White House. Mr. Nixon's only recent mention of the Vice President was a tepid birthday salute to Agnew at a GOP fund-raising dinner in Chicago. The President said that Agnew is "a man who is loyal, a man who is courageous, and a man who is competent at handling his duties at home and . . . with great dignity and great ability has represented America in 25 countries." Those who awaited a reference to "our next Vice President" didn't hear any. Mr. Agnew, however, has discussed his prospects with Republican congressmen and with several journalists. The thrust of his reported remarks has been that he doesn't really give a damn whether the President keeps him on the 1972 ticket and isn't wholly sure in his own mind that he wants to be kept on it. James Reston of *The New York Times,* a recent interviewer, perceived in the Vice President's indirectly quoted remarks an amiable candor and a refreshing willingness to bow out if that is the President's wish. Columnist Kevin Phillips, a former assistant to Attorney General Mitchell and a theologian of the Republican right, conveyed in an article that resulted in part from an interview with Agnew a note of whiny complaint that the Vice President had been forced into a role he never sought. His shouts for law-and-order, his attacks on the media, his view that aggressive dissent from adopted policy is an offensive mark of disrespect to the presidency itself, came through in the Phillips account (in *The New York Times Sunday Magazine*) as lines that the Vice President was required to take against his better judgment. Agnew's press spokesman, Victor Gold, said that this was Kevin Phillips and not Spiro Agnew talking. If so, Phillips could not have done Agnew any good with the President. The fact, surely as well known to Mr. Nixon as it is to his principal assistants, is that Agnew—denied, it's true, the part in policy formulation that he originally hoped for—welcomed the alternative role and has enjoyed his performance in it.

December 4, 1971

XXXVI

Talk and Travel

The consultations that the President is having between December 6 and January 7 with the chief executives of France and Portugal in the Azores, of Great Britain in Bermuda, and of Canada, West Germany, and Japan in Washington, Key Biscayne, and San Clemente, would have been arranged, though probably not concentrated in so short a period, even if Mr. Nixon were not going to Communist China next February and to Moscow in May. As the "White House official" whom attentive followers of the news have come to identify automatically with Henry Kissinger said aboard the President's airplane on the way back to Washington on November 28 from a four-day interlude in California, the world and the power relationships that dominate it are changing with unpredecented speed. The pace of change gives Mr. Nixon ample excuse to satisfy his itch for summitry and travel and, in the course of doing so, to appease the vanities and allay the concerns of other chiefs of state and government; capitalize upon the popular interest in his journeys to Peking and Moscow; and fortify himself for the presidential campaign in 1972.

The announcements on successive days, in Washington and California, of the preliminary journeys and consultations aroused a suspicion that the President was engaged in a transparent political and publicity ploy. He is surrounded by professional promoters who are prone to that sort of prostitution of large events, but the facts in this instance tell more about the nature of the world and its statesmen than the suspicion would if it were justified. Mr. Nixon originally intended to have his meetings with Pompidou of France, Caetano of Portugal, Heath of Great Britain, Brandt of West Germany, and Sato of Japan announced simultaneously, in one package. The meeting with Trudeau of Canada was an afterthought, initiated from Ottawa and squeezed into the schedule without great enthusiasm. At the last moment, in Thanksgiving week, the White House staff was made forcefully aware that a packaged announcement would offend the other conferees. They wanted inidividual notice, with due priority accorded the facts that President Pompidou was to be first and that Mr. Nixon was to be Prime Minister Heath's guest in British Bermuda. Prime Minister Colombo of Italy was omitted by mutual and thoroughly discussed agreement that the parliamentary and presidential elections in Italy in early December would introduce a period of prolonged uncertainty. Colombo or his successor may yet be favored with a Nixon meeting, before the President sets off for Peking in late February.

Although the December-January meetings are billed primarily as preludes to the Peking and Moscow trips, they also are intended to provide discussion of issues that are judged in themselves to require high-level consultation. A widely accepted impression is that they are particularly intended to give the President opportunity to pull back from the extreme positions taken and abrasively asserted by Secretary of the Treasury John B. Connally in the aftermath of Mr. Nixon's shattering blows on August 15 at the international monetary system and at the prevailing terms of international trade. His imposition of a 10 percent tariff surcharge on goods imported into the US and his suspension of the redemption of foreign-held dollars with gold did, among their other anticipated effects, disturb the political and diplomatic relations of the US with all of the governments involved in the coming round of talks. It is true as reported that the President's paramount security adviser, Henry Kissinger, has been telling Mr. Nixon that it's time for him to intervene personally and to soften the impact of the August actions. It is not true, as also reported, that Secretary Connally overplayed his hand and went beyond the President's intentions in demanding that other governments not only revalue their currencies to the US advantage but assume a greater share of the costs of allied defense and give US exporters a better break in their markets in return for removal of the 10 percent tariff surcharge. The President explicitly set forth those demands in his August speech and indicated that the surcharge would be lifted only when they were met to his satisfaction. His intention in the December-January meetings is not to repudiate Connally in any way. It is, on the contrary, to make the most of the shock that the President's August 15 announcements and Connally's aggressive implementation of them caused and, now that the desired effect has been had, to tie down and validate the compromises that are already in train. Kissinger's cautioning advice has run, not against the shock tactics in themselves, but against any temptation to let the tactics become permanent features of the administration's foreign policy and posture. As far back as last July, it may be worth noting in passage, Kissinger was known to feel at least as strongly as Connally does that such trading partners and competitors as Japan, France, and West Germany were getting a free ride in American markets at a no longer bearable degree of American expense and that, as both the President and his Treasury Secretary have been saying, it was time to even out the monetary, defense and trading imbalance in the non-Communist world.

The purpose of the consultations, such immediate issues aside, is to give the invited officials a sense of participation in the President's preparations for the Peking and Moscow visits. Very little of his substantive intentions can be imparted to the conferees that has not already been thrashed out with them in normal diplomatic exchange. But the process of personal consultation is designed to make them feel better about the exercise than they otherwise might. If it enables them to share a bit of the anticipated glory (as with Pompidou and Heath) or (as with Sato in Japan) to assure their restive home constituencies that their national interests have been taken into account, so much the better. If the preliminaries also diminish any hope in Peking and Moscow of creating new divisions or widening old ones between the US and what Mr. Nixon's press spokesman has been calling "our major allies," that will be accounted a worthwhile gain.

An incidental effect of the recent announcements has been to disclose a new arrangement between the President and Henry Kissinger. Three times since October, before and after his second exploratory visit to Peking and in conjunction with the announcement that Mr. Nixon will arrive there on February 21, Kissinger has talked to the press for quotation and on the record instead of holding to his previous practice of talking only "on background" and for attribution only to anonymous "White House officials." During an appearance on November 30, Kissinger called himself "a briefer who is very reluctant not to be identified," thus playing for the pleasure of reporters upon his reputation for pride in his expository prowess. His change of mode had actually been the subject of serious discussion with the President, who was persuaded that the previous Kissinger cover had been so thoroughly penetrated that any attempt to continue it as a regular practice would be futile and silly.

The essence of Kissinger's message on the Peking trip was that nothing much in the way of concrete and announced accomplishment should be expected. Nixon's unannounced hopes are a good deal more ambitious. For instance, no declared agreement upon a settlement of the Vietnam war or upon a ceasefire applying to all of Indochina is either expected or to be sought. But discussions that imaginably could lead to announced agreement on either or both scores two or three months after the visit are intended, and the preliminaries to just such discussions have been explored by Kissinger during his July and October visits to Peking and in other communication with Premier Chou En-lai. Similarly, there is no conceivable language in which the Peking leaders and Mr. Nixon could publicize any understanding that they may reach about the future status of the Republic of China on Taiwan. But an undeclared understanding, based upon mutual recognition of the certainty that Peking will never accept separate sovereignty for the Taiwan nationalists and that Mr. Nixon will not totally abandon them, is among the President's main objectives. Given that understanding, the goals of a negotiated accommodation between the Peking and Taiwan governments and of progress toward full and normal diplomatic relations between the US and the People's Republic should be attainable.

December 11, 1971

———

December 7 at the White House, and December 14 aboard the President's plane returning from the Azores, Kissinger reverted to "background" dissertations. Senator Goldwater put the December 7 transcript in the *Congressional Record* and *The Washington Post* broke the rule of confidence that was supposed to protect Kissinger from quotation of his in-flight remarks. On both occasions, he tried to pretty up the Administration's dismal handling of the India-Pakistan conflict and suggested that the Soviet government shared the onus for it with India. At the Azores conference with Pompidou, Nixon concluded and announced an agreement to devalue the American dollar in return for French trade and monetary concessions that Secretary Connally and his French counterparts were working out when the foregoing piece was written.

XXXVII

Lobbying Congress

The news that made Thursday, December 2, unique in the President's experience with Congress reached him in the following way. Max Friedersdorf, a White House lobbyist, telephoned the news of Mr. Nixon's third triumph of the day from the House of Representatives to John Nidecker, a junior assistant on the congressional liaison staff. Nidecker jotted "Metro vote—yeas 196, nays 183" on a slip of paper and dashed with it to the President's Oval Office. Admitted to the sanctum, Nidecker gave the note to Clark MacGregor, the Counsel for Congressional Relations. MacGregor read it and handed it to H. R. Haldeman, the President's chief of staff, who deemed it worthy of Mr. Nixon's attention and handed it to him. The President glanced at it and, without comment upon it or discerned reaction to it, proceeded with the business that was occupying him and a crowd of officials, reporters and cameramen who jammed his office.

Mr. Nixon's business at the moment was the induction of his new Secretary of Agriculture, Earl Butz. Messrs. Nixon and Butz agreed with each other that the President had made the best possible choice of a successor to the previous Secretary, Clifford Hardin, and that the Senate had acted with consummate wisdom in confirming the nomination. "You said you wanted an aggressive, articulate spokesman for agriculture in the White House and, Mr. President, you got him," Butz said to loud applause. The confirmation, voted four hours earlier by the narrow margin of 51 to 44, was the first of the Nixon victories in Congress that day. The second was the surrender of a House-Senate conference committee to the President's threat to veto a pending revenue bill unless the tax reductions provided in it were brought to a tolerable level and a proposal to finance the 1972 presidential campaign with public funds was eliminated. The "Metro vote" to release previously appropriated money for a local subway system was of immediate interest only to the city of Washington and to adjoining counties in Virginia and Maryland. But, for reasons to be explained, it was of great importance to Mr. Nixon. An examination of how the fights for the Butz nomination, the tax-bill changes and the subway money were waged from the White House should give some insight into how the President and the staff lobbyists who do most of the fighting for him deal with a Congress dominated by Democrats.

Clark MacGregor, the chief of the six working lobbyists, is a former Minnesota congressman. Largely at the instance of Attorney General John N. Mitchell, MacGregor ran for the Senate in 1970 and was defeated by Hubert Humphrey. After he was rewarded for his effort with the White House appointment, MacGregor at first went about his job with a show of corny fellowship that amused and repelled many of his former House colleagues. Then he settled down and has since been rated on Capitol Hill as a competent advocate of Nixon causes. His deputy, William Timmons, and the four assistants who do most of the floor work— Eugene Cowen and Tom Korologos in the Senate, Richard Cook and Max Friedersdorf in the House—came to the White House from the staffs of Republican senators, representatives and committee minorities. They are skilled in the ways of Congress and, judged on the total Nixon record, more effective than the harassment and opposition to be expected from the majority Democrats may indicate. But their overall effectiveness turns upon a factor that MacGregor and his assistants can't do much about. This

factor is their reputation in Congress for access to the President
and for being completely in his confidence.

The official claim is that MacGregor has sufficient access and
that he and his assistants have the prestige on Capitol Hill that
only it can give. Reporters who get around the Hill more than
I do tell me that this is not the impression they have from the
leading movers and shakers in Congress. It would be surprising
if it were. MacGregor's predecessor, Bryce Harlow, often seemed
to senators and representatives to be hurtfully remote from the
President although he had been associated with Nixon for many
years. The truth is that both the nature of Richard Nixon and the
organization of the Nixon White House deny the President's lobbyists the access and, what is more important, the reputation for
access that are essential if they are to accomplish all they are
expected to accomplish and, on occasion, catch hell for not ac-
complishing.

Mr. Nixon's lust for official privacy, the quality that his senior
assistants call "confidentiality," continues to restrict his range of
personal contact with the staff. A reason for this that is seldom
mentioned at the White House is the care taken by the guardian
of his time and energies, Bob Haldeman, to make sure that the
President is never pressed beyond the limits of his endurance.
Timmons, Cook and Cowen have all the contact they need with
the President's top assistants, individually and at the staff meetings
that begin each White House day. They rarely have direct contact
with the President, and their chief, MacGregor, is admitted to
the Nixon presence only when Haldeman allows. Haldeman is
sometimes depicted as the devil at the Nixon door, depriving the
President of needed contact and advice. MacGregor's subordinate
lobbyists don't see Haldeman that way. They are grateful for the
contact he permits their chief, for the efforts he makes to keep
them clued in with emerging policy decisions, and for the President's look of sustained health and vigor. They attribute this last
in part to the protection that Haldeman enforces.

Given the limitations, Mr. Nixon's lobbyists did well for him
in the Butz, tax and subway cases. Earl Butz seemed to have
everything going against him after the President nominated him
in the stated hope that he would be a more convincing and active

Secretary of Agriculture than Clifford Hardin had proved to be. Butz, an agricultural professor and school administrator by profession, was also a director of Ralston Purina and an owner of stocks in other big agricultural conglomerates. He seemed on his record to regard the growth of corporate farming and the erosion of the family farm so beloved of politicians with more tolerance and favor than are useful with the rural vote in election years. In a speech deriding Nixon welfare reform and other social measures in early 1971, he displayed a callous indifference to the needs of poor and hungry Americans. There was nothing for MacGregor, Cowen and Korologos to do but make the nomination a straight party issue of loyalty to the President, with side appeals to Democrats who had bigger fish than the Agriculture secretaryship, a job of waning importance, to fry. Gene Cowen's head count, put on paper an hour before the vote, had 51 Senators for Butz, 35 against him, and 10 doubtful. In the event, 14 Democrats voted with 37 Republicans to confirm Butz.

The tax and campaign funding issues became essentially questions of the President's credibility and the credibility of the staff lobbyists who, in the characteristic absence of direct intervention by him, had to speak for him. Was or wasn't Nixon bluffing when he had MacGregor announce that the President would surely veto the revenue bill if it came to him with more tax reductions than he thought wise and, in emphasized particular, if it promised the bankrupt Democrats a $20 million windfall of public funds in 1972? MacGregor, Cowen and Cook, the leaders in the lobby battle, relied mainly upon the details of the story they had to tell about how Nixon was brought to the unprecedented point of flatly guaranteeing a veto.

During Thanksgiving week, when the President was at his California home, the entire liaison staff united in arguing with the chief assistants that the threat of a veto was the only way a House-Senate conference committee could be persuaded to rewrite the bill to Nixon's satisfaction. On the Monday of the President's return to Washington, MacGregor had Attorney General Mitchell waiting at the White House. In a preparatory session with Mitchell, Gene Cowen said that in all the years of his congressional experience he had never known Senate and House Republicans to be as united on any issue as they were against the campaign-funding provision. The crass Democratic play for public help was more than some

Democrats could stomach. The capital's host of corporate lobbyists, gentry who seldom spend their credit with Congress on any issue not of primary concern to their employers, was lined up and ready to fight for tax reductions that would help business and against the proposed increase in those that would help individuals. So the chances of sustaining a veto were pretty good, if it came to that. Mitchell, persuaded, joined MacGregor and William Timmons in urging Nixon to guarantee the veto. He did, and the story of how he came to do it convinced the congressional skeptics that he really meant it. Wilbur Mills of Arkansas, the key conference committeeman, sponsored the desired cutback in tax reductions and came up with the campaign compromise, postponing help to Presidential candidates until 1976, that enabled Mr. Nixon to promise approval of the amended bill.

The subway story, briefly told, is simply that Mr. Nixon for once declared himself for something that was right because it was right and, in so doing, aligned himself with an unlikely coalition of House liberals and rank-and-filers who were fed up with arrogant leadership based upon seniority. A mobilization of local business and other factions comparable to the one for the tax-bill changes carried the day. When Clark MacGregor telephoned the President aboard his plane, winging him to Florida for a working weekend at his home there, and gave him the final vote (195–174), Mr. Nixon said "Congratulations" in a rather perfunctory tone. At this writing, his lobbyists have had no further word of thanks.

December 18, 1971

I was told after this piece appeared that a White House secretary took the telephoned Metro vote message from Friedersdorf and passed it to John Nidecker for delivery to MacGregor. Eugene Cowen resigned in mid-December to become a vice president of the American Broadcasting Companies, stationed in Washington.

XXXVIII

Shooting Santa Claus

As the afternoon of December 9 wore into dusk with no sign of an expected veto message from Mr. Nixon, the joke in the White House press room was that the President must be having a hard time making up his mind to shoot Santa Claus 16 days before Christmas. The bill that he had signaled his intention to veto extended the Economic Opportunity Act for two years, established a National Legal Services Corporation to help poor people, and authorized the expenditure of $2 billion a year for "comprehensive child development programs, including a full range of health, education and social services." Congress had just decided by large majorities that these federal services were "essential to the achievement of the full potential of the nation's children" and should be made available to children from the womb to age 14 "regardless of economic, social and family backgrounds." This part of the bill was, as Mr. Nixon was about to say, a truly radical departure from the concept that only children of the very poor deserve and require federal care of the proscribed kind, on a much more modest scale than was now proposed.

With the approach of 6 P.M., three hours after reporters had been alerted to stand by for the veto message, the consensus among them was that the President had contrived to shoot down the bill too late for any but brief and superficial exposure of the deed on the evening news shows. That was the result, but evidence that it was not intended was fairly persuasive. It was said that Mr. Nixon got a final whack at the draft of the message late in a busy day. His determination to veto the bill was already known and had been denounced by advocates of expanded child care. Two assistants who would have had to have a hand in deliberate delay, Press Secretary Ronald Ziegler and Patrick Buchanan, who wrote the draft, were observed by associates to have been dismayed and irritated by foul-ups in retyping and reproduction of the veto text after the President scribbled his last changes.

The most interesting aspect of the veto message, considering the prior knowledge that it was to be issued, was its demonstration of Mr. Nixon's talent for messing up a basically defensible position with extraneous assertions that reflect his worst characteristics and indicate obeisance to the worst elements in his national constituency. This the President accomplished with his concluding statement that the proposed expansion of federal care programs "would commit the vast authority of the national government to the side of communal approaches to child rearing over against the family-centered approach." None of the administration witnesses who opposed various parts of the vetoed bill during committee hearings raised that objection. Mr. Nixon's resort to it was a straight echo of Vice President Agnew, who began suggesting in November that comprehensive child care on the proposed scale was a notion borrowed from Communist Russia and exploited by professional American behaviorists who yearned to precondition and control the attitudes of everybody from kindergarten tots to public officials. Senator Strom Thurmond of South Carolina held forth to the same effect in a floor speech from which Pat Buchanan, one of Mr. Nixon's more conservative assistants, might have lifted the "communal" and similar passages in the veto message. They opened the President to the charge, promptly made by critics of the veto, that the entire action was a patent and unjustified concession to know-nothing rightists to whom Mr. Nixon must look for support in 1972.

There were better arguments against all three of the vetoed bill's major components. It was quite true, as the President said and as wiser advocates of his policies maintained during the committee hearings, that the enacted measure burdened the Office of Economic Opportunity, the projected legal services corporation, and the child-care program with administrative complexities and inhibitions that were likely to diminish their usefulness. Early in his term, Mr. Nixon announced his wish to make OEO an experimental and innovative rather than an operating agency by delegating its authority to manage proven poverty programs to such federal departments as Labor and Health, Education, and Welfare. For the first time since the Economic Opportunity Act was passed in 1964, Congress voted in this bill to deny him the power of delegation. It also tied so much of the authorized funds to programs specified by Congress that OEO would have lost essential flexibility and would have been short of money to pay for needed research and experimentation. The President believably said that he would have vetoed an OEO extension that came separately to him with these restrictions in it. As it happened, and as his official spokesmen did not seem to know, the veto did not imperil OEO as it presently functions. Money for it was provided in a supplemental appropriation and authority to spend the money in the current fiscal year survives from the original Economic Opportunity Act.

The legal services corporation would have absorbed some 930 state and local legal services programs now financed and supervised by OEO. Mr. Nixon had proposed and continued to insist that he alone choose the directors who would run the corporation, subject to confirmation of their appointments by the Senate. Congress preferred and tried to impose upon him an unwieldy method of choosing 11 of 17 directors from lists submitted to the President by the US Judicial Conference, the American and National (all-black) Bar Associations, and organizations representing trial lawyers and supporters, attorneys and clients of the legal services program. National leaders of the entire organized bar endorsed the enacted proposal, although some of them were dubious about the complexities. Mr. Nixon was entitled to his own doubts, but he carried them to the point of absurdity when he said in the veto

message that "it would be better to have no legal services corporation than one so irresponsibly structured." Here again, he opened
himself to the suspicion, already prevalent among advocates of
federally provided legal services for the poor, that he was more
interested in minimizing their capacity to upset the non-poor with
aggressive court actions than he was in assuring justice for the
poor.

Before Mr. Nixon introduced his nonsense about "communal"
subversion of family rights and responsibilities, a charge that might
as well be addressed to the public schools as to expanded child-
care programs, the main issue between the administration and such
supporters of comprehensive care as Senator Walter Mondale of
Minnesota was administrative practicability. Elliot Richardson, the
Secretary of Health, Education, and Welfare, and the subordinate
officials who testified at congressional hearings made a good case
for their claim that the proposal to have the federal government
deal directly with and supervise upwards of 7000 "prime sponsors"
and many thousands more of local contractors, public and private,
who would administer individual projects was inherently unwork-
able. Richardson's proposal, later modified, to restrict the prime
sponsors to state and big-city governments was extreme on its side.
But the issue could have been reasonably compromised if Mondale
in the Senate, Representative John Brademas in the House, and
their supporting colleagues had not been as insistent as they were
that the principle of local initiative and parental participation be
taken to the extreme that they advocated. On cost, the Administration and the expansionists were not as far apart as they appeared to be. The administration claim that the cost could run to
$20 billion a year was a calculated exaggeration, but Senator
Mondale said during debate that it could rise to $7 billion annually
within four years.

Larger issues underlay those of management and cost, and upon
them the advocates of expanded child care were unassailably right.
One of these basic issues was what to do about the immense
changes in a society in which the proportion of mothers who work
for pay is expected to increase from 10 percent in 1940 to 70
percent in 1980. Another was the validity of Mr. Nixon's view,
expressed in his welfare reform bill, that the primary purpose of
federally financed child care is to justify forcing welfare mothers
to leave their homes and children and work for their livings. Mr.

Nixon, seeing in comprehensive care a plot to communize American life, is trying to preserve a society that was beginning to vanish when he began his climb to the presidency 25 years ago.

December 25, 1971

XXXIX

Toilet Training

The recent rumpus over the use and abuse of "background" news cannot be intelligibly discussed without reference to the toilet situation aboard Air Force One, a conveyance that I refuse to join Mr. Nixon in calling the Spirit of '76. Most of the people who travel on the President's plane ride in the staff compartment between his private quarters and the rear section. The only facility available to them is opposite the space in the rear section where a press pool of five reporters and three photographers is seated. Mere rank, it must be understood, does not admit anybody on the plane to the President's territory. This means that Cabinet officers and staff assistants of high and low degree must either exert remarkable control or confront the pool reporters at some point during all but the shortest flights. Press Secretary Ronald Ziegler acknowledged that he had the resultant problem in mind when he said at the White House on December 15 that "Government officials who are on board Air Force One and accompanying the President feel that they are somewhat limited, or hesitate to a great extent, walking to the press area because they feel they are going to be driven into an immediate press conference situation."

Now for some necessary definitions and a few opinions before we get to the core of the story. The press pool on Air Force One is chosen by the White House press staff. It is limited in number because space on the plane is limited. The pool is the agent of all the publications and electronic media represented by the scores of other reporters, photographers and technicians who travel on a chartered press plane, usually preceding the President to his destination and following him back to Washington. By old and generally accepted custom, all of the represented media are bound by whatever rules the pool on a given flight may accept when the conditions governing the use of information imparted on the plane are laid down either by the official source or by the accompanying press officer. Very little on-the-record information, attributable to a named source, is provided on presidential flights. On many flights, none at all is provided. When information is offered in flight, it is usually under one of three rules that also govern much of the news provided in Washington. News provided on a "background" basis may be attributed to an unnamed official or to unnamed officials and the place where they work (White House, State Department, etc.) may be identified. "Deep background" news may be attributed only to unnamed official sources, without mention of any place or agency. And there is "the Lindley rule," formulated by and named for Ernest K. Lindley, a former Washington correspondent and State Department official. Under it, no attribution of any kind is permitted. A reporter either uses the information on his own authority or doesn't use it. In Washington and elsewhere, these rules are the subjects of perennial complaint by reporters and editors who feel that the background device in its various forms is misused and abused by officials. Indeed it is, for everything from plain lying to the flotation of trial balloons. This fact notwithstanding, I have no sympathy for the complainants. Reporters and editors who let themselves and their publications be "used" by backgrounding officials in a wrongful way have only themselves to blame. Reporters and editors who can't spot the lies and prick the balloons shouldn't be in the news business. Colleagues who are under greater competitive pressures than I am tell me that this is a sanctimonious attitude, irrelevant to their situation and problems. Maybe so. But it's my attitude and I stick to it.

Now to the story. The most skillful backgrounder in Washington and one of the most frequent visitors to the rear section of the

President's plane is Henry A. Kissinger, the assistant for national security affairs. Kissinger and the President recently agreed that his background cover had been blown so often that he should do more talking on the record and less in concealment. But our Henry just loves to background: the practice gives play to his wit, feeds his abundant vanity, and in his opinion serves essential purposes of diplomacy. When Kissinger encountered the pool reporters on the afternoon of December 14, flying home from Mr. Nixon's conference in the Azores with President Pompidou of France, the conflict between India and Pakistan and the Administration's sorry role in it were much on the minds of the journalists. The subject was especially on the mind of David J. Kraslow of *The Los Angeles Times,* who had reported in his paper that morning that the Indo-Pakistan affair had occupied more of Nixon's and Pompidou's time than the official accounts indicated. Both Kraslow and Kissinger said later that Kissinger appeared in the pool area at the reporters' insistent demand and that his remarks were offered in answer to extremely persistent questioning. Assuming this to be so, what happened on the plane and afterward is all the more extraordinary. The least to be said about it is that Kissinger, with the President's knowledge, used to the utmost an opportunity that was forced upon him.

The key section of the customary pool report, typed out by Kraslow and photocopied aboard the plane for distribution to the general press upon arrival in Washington, was preceded with the following notation: "Lindley rule—deep background: it was the pool's impression that the information in this category could be written on our own without attribution to any administration official—at least that is what we understood Kissinger to have in mind." Kissinger had this in mind because he was dealing with what the Administration believed to be the Soviet Union's calculated support of India and deliberate refusal to help the US government bring about a cease-fire. This view had already been conveyed to the press, though not in a way that could be attributed to any responsible official. In a passage that will figure in the diplomatic history of the time, the pool report continued: "Asked what the Soviet motive is in its behavior on the India-Pak (*sic*) war, Kissinger said it is apparently to humiliate China—to show to the world that China cannot prevent what is happening in Pakistan. Asked if there is a danger of the South Asian situation deteriorating to the point that it might affect the President's plans to visit Moscow, Kissinger said not yet but that we would have to wait to see what happens in the next few days. Asked if we should infer from that statement that if the Russians didn't begin to exercise a restraining influence (on India) very soon, the plans for the President's trip might be changed, Kissinger said in such an event the entire matter might well be reexamined. He said the US is definitely looking to the Soviets to become a restraining influence in (the) next few days. But if the Russians continue to deliberately encourage military actions, a new look might have to be taken at the President's summitry plans."

Kraslow sent the typed original to Kissinger, for his review and approval. Kissinger changed the statement that "the entire matter might well be reexamined" to read, "the entire US-Soviet relationship might well be reexamined."

Here was an attempt to have the press report on its own authority, with no citation of any official source, a threat to the Soviet leaders whom Mr. Nixon hopes to cultivate in Moscow next May. It was too much for *The Washington Post,* which in a front-page story identified Kissinger and quoted the pool's version of his remarks. The *Post* justified its violation of the rules with a pious blast at the background process: "We are now convinced that we have engaged in this deception and done this disservice to the reader long enough." This noble sentiment was followed by a brilliant piece of *Post* reporting, simultaneously noting and puncturing the Administration's background claims to have whipped the Soviet Union into line and to have brought about the India-Pakistan cease-fire. The *Post* account relied almost entirely upon background information dug out by its reporters on their promise not to identify the sources. Kissinger plugged the Administration claims in backgrounders for Associated Press and United Press International reporters. John Scali, a former TV correspondent who works at the White House, briefed reporters who couldn't get to Kissinger. At the State Department, Assistant Secretary Joseph Sisco did his bit for the Nixon line. It was all done at Mr. Nixon's order. "High administration officials" had their day in the national press and—who knows?—they probably were telling part of the truth.

January 1 and 8, 1972

XL

After
Three Years

Here is one observer's appraisal of Richard Nixon at the start of his fourth year in the presidency. The reader is warned that it is going to be an unsatisfactory appraisal, soggy with ambivalence and short of certainties. There was so much to like and so much to dislike in what Mr. Nixon did during this third year in the office, and there continued to be so little to like in him as a person, that in this season of judgment I find myself incapable of the firm and rounded judgments that more fortunate journalists seem to render with ease.

Let us begin with the man. At the end of his first year Mr. Nixon seemed to me to have shown himself to be a better man than he had previously permitted himself to be and a better President than he appeared likely to be in his 1968 campaign. His second year inspired the conclusion that his wild swings from sober and often admirable proposals to raucous appeals to the basest instincts of the electorate made confidence in his fundamental integrity and good faith impossible. At the close of the third year and the beginning of the fourth, Mr. Nixon comes across to me as a President who, in defensive response to the negative view, has constructed a false image of himself and has persuaded himself that it is the true image. Bits of evidence in support of this impression are scattered through a series of magazine and television interviews and performances that were arranged for the President in late 1971 and early 1972.

These exposures reflected a return to the theory, thought by some of his associates to have been proven incorrect in early 1971, that he would appear to the public to be a warm and likeable fellow if he parted the curtain of privacy he kept around himself and let others see him as his assistants see him. It was tried and it didn't work very well; the verdict of the professional imagists who serve him was that Mr. Nixon did himself more harm than good when he tried to loosen up and be his allegedly natural self in group and individual interviews. In late 1971, with the year for reelection approaching, he and his polishers decided to try it again, in a big way. NBC televised parts of a Nixon working day. CBS broadcast a pre-Christmas romp with the President's dogs, wife, daughters and sons-in-law. Time's editors, its White House correspondent and Dan Rather of CBS interviewed him. On the whole, Mr. Nixon came off quite well. But there were little touches, petty flaws and contradictions, that in their way were as revealing as the passages—and there were many—in which the President appeared to be credible and likeable.

On the NBC show, the President telephoned Congressman Wilbur Mills and said that he was calling because "I thought there was a lousy story (about Mills) in the papers this morning." Mr. Nixon told Jerrold Schecter of Time that "I don't worry about the press . . . I never start the morning by reading through The Washington Post and The New York Times." (Technically true; he said in the same interview that he gets his news from a summary prepared by his staff.) Nixon to Schecter on how he treats his assistants: "If anybody does anything for me that I've asked him to do, I support him totally. Nobody is ever dressed down for making a mistake." Nixon to Mills on how they should work together to reconcile their different revenue-sharing bills: ". . . if you find any of our people that are giving you trouble on this, if they are getting out of line, you let me know." Nixon told Schecter that "The first rule of leadership is to save yourself for the big decisions. Don't let your mind become cluttered with trivia." NBC's viewers saw and heard Nixon rebuking an assistant for proposing that the President give signed photographs to heads of state and government with whom he was about to confer and dramatically scratching out a reference to photographs in a script prepared for the meetings. Nixon spoke at length of a President's need to be cool and disciplined, ever prepared for the "great decisions," and remarked that "I have my moments when I'm not as disciplined as I might be, but I try to overcome them." His preoccupation with the point suggested that he depicts himself to himself as a cooler and more disciplined President than he really is.

Nixon's assertions that he wouldn't "engage in any political activities" until after the 1972 Republican convention were something more than the usual guff of a President who is running for reelection. They were the effusions of a President who has convinced himself that he isn't engaging in politics when he departs from habit and grabs at chances for extra magazine and television exposure and sees to it that the TV networks have the opportunity for maximum coverage of his summit visits to Peking and Moscow. He said he realized that "anyone who sits in this office is going to be charged with having a political motivation for everything that he does." Pleading innocence, he had the air of a man who believes himself innocent. Insisting in early January that he hadn't finally decided to run for reelection, the President was assumed to be building interest in his promised announcement of that "very important decision." It could be that Nixon has come to think of himself as a President who actually is, as he said he was, capable of choosing not to run again. He would figure, if I read him rightly, that he could enter the Republican primaries and still choose not to stand for renomination at the convention. An announcement that committed him only to enter the primaries and left the ultimate option intact without disclosing it would be in character.

The President was at his best and most appealing when Dan Rather, in the course of a memorable display of inquisitorial courtesy and toughness, put it to him that pollers find a lot of people thinking he "failed to inspire confidence and faith and lacked personal warmth and compassion." Rather asked, "Why do you suppose that is?" and Nixon answered: "Well, it is because people tell the pollster that. So that must be what the people believe. . . . I would simply answer the question by saying that my strong point is not rhetoric, it isn't showmanship, it isn't big promises—those things that create the glamor and excitement that people call charisma and warmth. My strong point, if I have a strong point, is performance. I always do more than I say. Oh, I don't mean that from time to time I may not have made promises that I was unable to keep, but, generally speaking . . . I believe that actions are what count."

Here, it seems to me, we have a President who has trained himself not to give a damn about "what the people believe" about him as a person. Giving a damn about it would be too painful, too much of a drain upon inner resources. For such a man, there is a cathartic relief in feeling free to say as he said to *Time's* editors, at a risk surely understood, that "black people are different from white people" and (to Rather) that women will have to "develop respect for themselves as executives rather than as women" before they can expect to rise in business and politics and, some day, see a woman in the presidency. Mr. Nixon's seizure of every opportunity to emphasize the work requirement in his welfare reform bill and to portray, with cynical falsity, the run of people on welfare as fakes and free-loaders is generally taken to be a means of appealing to voters who feel the same way. It is that. But it also is a reflection of Nixon himself, of the mean and cruel streak in him that flashes into view (as it occasionally did during NBC's working day with him) when the Nixon mouth turns down and the Nixon voice roughens.

Showmanship and big promises indeed are not the President's strong points. His attempts at showmanship and his indulgence in big promises are among his weak points. His 1971 State of the Union Message, the one that proclaimed his "new American Revolution," was a monster of a promise, and it was followed by a lackadaisical effort to fulfill it. And yet—here comes the acknowledged ambivalence—the message and the legislative proposals that rather feebly implemented it set in motion and stimulated trends that eventually will change and improve our national life. A necessary sharing of federal revenues with needy state and local governments is going to come about—not as soon as the President promised and not in the forms he suggested, but sooner and to better effect than the critics who have pronounced his program dead suppose. National health insurance is on the way, in part because the President embraced the principle in a stingy fashion. An Environmental Protection Agency is in being and at work,

208 NIXON WATCH III

inhibited to some extent by the politics of privilege but nevertheless expressive of a federal commitment to the proposition that only federal power can compel us to save ourselves. A federally guaranteed income for people who cannot earn it for themselves is in the offing, largely at the instance of a President who professes to detest the concept of a guaranteed income. A capitalist economy that was headed into disastrous inflation at the beginning of 1971 is under the restraints of federal wage and price controls imposed by a President who was saying at mid-year that he would never impose them. A conservative President is accused by conservative supporters of cloaking liberal measures in conservative rhetoric and the accusation, allowing for some exaggeration of the liberal content, is so well founded that Mr. Nixon hardly bothers to deny its truth.

The fourth year began with the President saying that the peace issue will be his winning issue in 1972. His dismal dealings with the conflict between India and Pakistan suggested a failure of calculation and judgment that, if repeated, could mar the prospect. But, except there and in Indochina, where the President continued to trap himself with his refusal to accept the fact of defeat in any form that might be perceived as defeat, the foreign policy performance in 1971 justified the prediction. Mr. Nixon was believable when he said that he sees in himself a President who is in office at a point in time when it may be possible to do more than any President before him could do to promote a realistic and stable realignment of the world power structure. He was credible, he almost persuaded, when he said that his highest purpose "in the brief time I have" is to grasp the discerned opportunity and so make a difference for his country and for the world that may long outlast him.

January 15, 1972

The day this piece came off *The New Republic* presses, the President announced that he was "a candidate for re-nomination and re-election."

INDEX